Does Perstempo Hurt Reenlistment?

The Effect of Long or Hostile Perstempo on Reenlistment

James Hosek
Mark Totten

Prepared for the
Office of the Secretary of Defense

National Defense Research Institute

RAND

Many people think of future defense challenges solely in terms of evolving threats, new technologies, and defense budgets, often paying scant attention to the crucial role of defense manpower. But manpower constitutes a vital element of the nation's defense capability, one that must be sustained if tomorrow's force is to be ready for the wide set of contingencies currently envisioned in the post–Cold War world.

We are seeing the strains of adapting to this world. The services now face an increased pace of activity in peacetime operations such as peacekeeping and humanitarian assistance, the ever-present possibility of major theater war, and the looming potential for increased terrorism. In the realm of defense manpower, the increase in peacetime operations has generated concern that personnel are being used too intensively and might therefore be subject to high stress, decreased morale, and reduced family stability, resulting in lower retention. Moreover, these outcomes might create difficulty in recruiting, further worsening the potentially negative impact on readiness.

This analysis focuses on a key aspect of these concerns: the effect of recent personnel tempo, or perstempo, on reenlistment. The analysis helps reconcile the prospect of decreased reenlistment with the contrary view that perstempo actually has benefited reenlistment. The findings provide insight into the relationship between perstempo and reenlistment and the consequences of possibly higher future perstempo for reenlistment. In addition, the analysis offers several new measures of perstempo and a theoretical framework for considering perstempo.

The report should interest members of the defense policy community concerned with the topics of perstempo, readiness, and retention; it also will interest members of the policy research community who are concerned with data, models, and methods related to those topics.

This research was conducted for RAND's National Defense Research Institute Advisory Board. NDRI is a federally funded research and development center sponsored by the Office of the Secretary of Defense, the Joint Staff, the unified commands, and the defense agencies.

CONTENTS

FIGURES

TABLES

We analyze whether long separation or hostile duty affect the reenlistment of active duty enlisted personnel. Long separation and hostile duty are elements of personnel tempo, or perstempo. Motivation for the analysis comes from concern that current levels and patterns of perstempo can have, and may already have had, an adverse effect on reenlistment. Today's perstempo reflects a strategic posture under which the United States engages peace operations and continues to base troops abroad for regional stability, prevention of wider conflict, and long-term environment-shaping. In conducting this research we developed new measures of perstempo, placed perstempo within a theory of retention, performed statistical analyses of the effect of long or hostile duty on reenlistment, and considered the policy implications of our findings.

KEY FINDINGS

Does long or hostile duty increase reenlistment? The answers are yes and no. For personnel who have had no long or hostile duty, gaining some is predicted to increase reenlistment. For those who have had long or hostile duty, adding more will tend to reduce reenlistment, especially if the additional duty is hostile. These findings apply primarily to first-term personnel, and suggest that while long or hostile duty is a "good thing," there can be too much of a good thing, particularly if it involves danger.

In addition, we highlight several other findings:

- Despite the increase in perstempo occurring since the Gulf War, the level of long or hostile duty in 1993–1995 did not reduce but increased first-term reenlistment in the Army and Marine Corps compared to what reenlistment would have been in the absence of such duty. Long or hostile duty had little effect on first-term reenlistment in the Navy and Air Force.

- For early-career personnel (beyond first term but with 10 or fewer years of service), long or hostile duty in 1993–1995 increased reenlistment in all four services.

- Since having some long or hostile duty tends to increase reenlistment but having "too much" can decrease reenlistment, our findings imply the value of balancing the burden of long or hostile duty among service members.

- Since service members choose their service and occupation in part on the basis of expectations about long or hostile duty, it is important to establish accurate expectations about the incidence, extent, and nature of such duty. Accurate expectations reduce the chance of adverse surprises—that is, having far more or far less long or hostile duty than expected—that can reduce reenlistment.

MEASURES OF PERSTEMPO

Measures of recruit quality, attrition, and retention have become commonplace, but not so measures of perstempo. Therefore, as a first step we constructed measures of long or hostile duty. The measures are based on two special pays: Family Separation Allowance, paid to personnel with dependents when the personnel are separated from their dependents for 30 consecutive days or longer, and, to a far lesser extent, paid to service members who must establish a second residence when based abroad; and Hostile Fire Pay, paid to personnel subject to hostile fire or explosion or on duty in areas deemed hostile. Family Separation Allowance and Hostile Fire Pay are each paid on a monthly basis according to the same criteria across all four services. We refer to separations of 30 days or more as "long," and duty in which Hostile Fire Pay is received as "hazardous" or "hostile."

Using the Perstempo file from the Defense Manpower Data Center (DMDC), we constructed four measures of long or hostile duty. Two measures are *group monthly rates*, and two measures are individual-member-level counts of months and episodes of long or hostile duty *over a 24-month period*. The individual measures add detail to the group picture; the monthly rates do not indicate whether personnel with long or hostile duty in a given month have had such duty recently, for how long, and how many times. The measures are:

- *Long or hostile duty—unit:* the monthly rate associated with unit separation/deployment, e.g., the unit may be stationed abroad on an unaccompanied tour, afloat on a sea tour, or deployed on a peace operation. (This measure is based on a variable created by DMDC.)

- *Long or hostile duty—total:* the monthly rate inclusive of unit and individual (nonunit) duty. Service members may have long or hostile duty even though their unit does not.

- *Months of long or hostile duty:* a service member's total months of long or hostile duty over 24 months.

- *Episodes of long or hostile duty:* a service member's separate episodes of long or hostile duty over 24 months.

As a set, the measures effectively describe various dimensions of long or hostile duty. However, the measures have several limitations. The group measure undercounts Marine Corps unit duty. The months and episodes measures undercount long, *nonhostile* months and episodes. More generally, the data do not account for short nonhostile duty, where short means less than 30 days; the frequency of action (e.g., number of missions) during a month when duty is indicated; the intensity of activity (e.g., hours per day); and specific conditions such as actual combat, adverse weather, rough terrain, poisonous wildlife, toxic substances, disease, and chemical or biological weapons.

FINDINGS

Monthly Rate

- The total rate exceeds the unit rate for the Army and Air Force, but the two rates are similar for the Navy. Since FY 1988, the beginning of our data, the total rate has been 1.5 to 2 times higher than the unit rate in the Army and 2 times higher in the Air Force. The Army tailor-makes task forces, filling them with the appropriate specializations and experience by drawing soldiers from various units. The Air Force frequently flies missions involving part, but not all, of a wing. Therefore, a focus on unit deployments would seriously understate the overall level of long or hostile duty for these services. However, the total and unit rates show little difference for the Navy, because all members of a Navy unit embark when a vessel deploys, and personnel from other units are rarely attached to the deploying unit. The Marine Corps appears to have a large difference between the total and unit rates, but this is a mirage caused by the undercount of unit long or hostile duty.

- Total rates remained fairly constant at about 13 percent for the Navy and 17 percent for the Marine Corps over 1987–1996, apart from increases driven by the Gulf War and Somalia. Rates rose for the Army from 5–7 percent before the war to 8–10 percent after, and rose sharply to 13 percent in 1995–1996 because of Bosnia. Air Force rates more than doubled from around 3 percent before the Gulf War to 6–7 percent after the war.

- Much of the growth in Army and Air Force total rates can be traced to increases in hostile duty. For the most part, the increase in Army hostile duty comes from long (30 days or more) deployments to hostile areas, whereas much of the Air Force's increase comes from multiple short deployments or missions to hostile areas.

- Although the Navy and Marine Corps showed relatively less change in the total rate, the mix of duty in both services shifted markedly toward hostile duty. The data reflect that Navy vessels, with Marine units on board, were underway in hostile waters.

- When total rates were examined at the broadest occupation levels, we found similar increases across occupations. The increases were most similar in the Navy and Marine Corps, where different specialties are affected by the same vessel manning and support policies, and more diverse in the Army and Air Force.

Months and Episodes

- The percentages of personnel experiencing some long or hostile duty over a 24-month period appear strikingly higher than the monthly rates. For first-term personnel, 24-month rates were: Army—39 percent, Air Force—31 percent, Navy—69 percent, and Marine Corps—61 percent. For early careerists—those beyond the first term and with 10 or fewer years of service—the rates were: Army—44 percent, Air Force—37 percent, Navy—69 percent, and Marine Corps—48 percent. In other words, the 24-month rates were three to five times higher than the monthly rates.

- Further, among personnel who had long or hostile duty assignments over a 24-month period, one-third to two-thirds of the episodes were hostile.

The 24-month rates were computed only for 1993–1995 because of data limitations. Further, the rates were computed only for personnel facing a reenlistment decision in the period from July 1995–June 1996, because the 24-month variables on months and episodes are used in the analysis of reenlistment. However, we expect the rates to be accurate overall estimates for other first-term personnel (who are not in initial training) and other career personnel.

Perstempo and Reenlistment

The analysis of long or hostile duty asked whether a service member's cumulative experience—months or episodes during a 24-month window—affected the probability of reenlistment. The analysis accounted for the service member's AFQT category, level of education, gender, race/ethnicity, and occupation; separate reenlistment models were fit for first-term and early-career personnel in each of the four services. We found:

- That long or hostile duty affects reenlistment, and the effects are stronger among first-term personnel than early-career personnel.

- Three distinct elements of the effect of *months* of duty on reenlistment. First, compared with service members who had no months of such duty, those who had months were initially (i.e., for low months) more likely to reenlist. Second, as the number of months increased, the likelihood of reenlisting decreased. Third, the decrease was more rapid for hostile months than for nonhostile months. The size of these effects varied across the services and by first-term/early-career status.

- That *episodes* showed a pattern of response that depended on the number of hostile and nonhostile episodes. Having a single nonhostile episode clearly raised the reenlistment probability, compared to having no episodes. However, having a single hostile episode resulted in a reenlistment probability about the same as that for having no episodes. Generally, the reenlistment probability rose with the number of episodes if they were all nonhostile, but the more often the episodes were hostile the more the rate flattened or declined.

POLICY EXERCISES

We used the regression-analysis results to predict the extent to which long or hostile duty levels in the mid-1990s (1993–1995) had a net positive or negative effect on reenlistment of personnel who had such duty. For first-term personnel, we found the following changes in reenlistment: Army—18 percent increase; Marine Corps—6 percent increase; Navy and Air Force—1 percent decrease. For early-career personnel, we found: Army—6 percent increase; Marine Corps—10 percent increase; Navy—8 percent increase; and Air Force—10 percent increase.

For the Army, Air Force, and Marine Corps, we predicted the change in reenlistment resulting from adding one more hostile episode, or alternatively, three more months of long or hostile duty. This was computed separately for nonhostile and hostile months. Further, because the effect of adding months differs between personnel who have had none and those who already had positive long or hostile duty, predictions were made separately for these groups. The results vary by case, but we found that adding a hostile episode to first-term Army personnel who have already had one or more episodes of either kind would reduce their reenlistment probability from .45 to .40, a 10-percent drop; the corresponding figures for the Marine Corps are .24 to .20, a 16-percent drop.

In short, more hostile activity takes a toll on retention. To put this in perspective, these decreases in reenlistment are larger than what could be expected from a 5-percent cut in military pay relative to civilian pay, which would be considered a large cut.

No change in reenlistment is predicted for the Air Force, but this finding must be viewed cautiously because of the data limitations: the lack of control for the intensity of action within a month—e.g., number of missions flown—and the pace of operations, which affects both deploying personnel and the nondeploying personnel who support them.

Because the Navy can handle peace operations such as those experienced since the Gulf War by repositioning vessels already deployed, we did not consider adding an episode or adding three months of long or hostile duty. Instead, we examined the effect on reenlistment of reducing months among Navy personnel who had the highest number of months. Such a change might be implemented by keeping fewer deployed vessels from exceeding the Navy's guideline for 180-day deployments. When the number of months of personnel who were in the highest 20 percent of accumulated hostile months were reduced to the average number of months for the next highest 20 percent, reenlistment increased by 7.5 percent for affected first-term personnel, from 40 to 43 percent. The increase in reenlistment for early-career personnel was negligible, however. Also, the policy of capping nonhostile months had virtually no effect on first-term or early-career reenlistment.

THEORY

Because personnel tempo has emerged as a significant defense manpower issue, the need for a theory regarding its effects on personnel has become important. A theory of perstempo can provide an effective way to describe how deployment can alter reenlistment and factors such as choice of service, choice of occupation, speed of promotion, one's effort to change probability of deployment, the impact of changes in workload, and changes in contingent pay. A theory can attempt to combine these into a logical framework for how to maximize reenlistment wherein individuals may differ in their taste for military service, ability, and risk aversion; it may also account for the variation of their circumstances across occupations and across different kinds of separation or deployment experiences. Such a model could enable policymakers to test or simulate the effects of policy changes by varying its elements.

This report takes the first steps toward constructing such a theory. The approach builds on a rich existing theory treating retention within a dynamic framework that allows for differences in individual preferences, ability, and effort.

POLICY IMPLICATIONS

Several policy implications emerge from the analysis.

Measurement methods matter. Long or hostile duty—total reveals significantly higher monthly rates than long or hostile duty—unit. Further, 24-month rates reveal that, even at seemingly low monthly rates, large proportions of personnel are directly involved in long or hostile duty within a two-year window. Also, units deployed to hostile areas must be supported by those at home bases; hence, deployment involves a considerable portion of the force. Clearly, perstempo measures can be improved. Improvements include capturing accurate information on short perstempo; total versus unit separation or deployment; specifics about the nature of the deployment such as weather, terrain, combat, or disease; information about the impact on dependents, as well as the efficacy of family-support programs and networks; and impact on nondeployed personnel.

Does long or hostile duty increase reenlistment? Our results imply that, initially, having some long or hostile duty tends to increase reenlistment, especially for first-term personnel. However, adding further long *or* hostile duty will incrementally reduce reenlistment, and the rate of decline is faster if the duty is hostile. Also, depending on the amount of prior long or hostile duty and on the amount added, reenlistment could be driven to a level below what it would have been in the absence of such duty. Finally, early-career personnel are not impervious to changes in perstempo: while having some long or hostile duty increases their reenlistment compared with having no such duty, additional hostile duty will reduce their reenlistment from that higher level. Extensive additional hostile duty could reduce their reenlistment below what it would have been in the absence of long or hostile duty.

Where is the margin? The pace of peacetime operations involving hazardous duty is greater in the 1990s than it was in the 1980s. Our results indicate that the higher levels of separation and deployment prevailing in 1993–1995 had relatively little negative impact on reenlistment, and for many personnel—those with nonhostile duty—the impact was positive. The pace of peace operations has not slackened; considering the multiyear U.S. presence in Bosnia, involvement in humanitarian and disaster-relief operations, and still other operations, today's perstempo could be having a less positive, and even a negative, impact on retention (as future research can reveal). We found that the impact of added long or hostile duty differs for personnel who have had it from those who have not, and whether it is hostile or nonhostile. Thus, if the added hostile duty can be spread to troops who have not yet been deployed, then the effect on reenlistment is likely to be positive; if the added duty falls to those who have already been deployed, then the effect on reenlistment is likely to be negative. Of course, decisions about how to allocate additional assignments must include a variety of factors beyond effects on retention rates. A service's capability to share long or hostile duty among units may be influenced by advantages gained from assigning certain units particular roles for a major theater war and assuring that these units stand at full readiness. For readiness reasons, it may not be advisable to spread such duty more broadly.

ACKNOWLEDGMENTS

We greatly appreciate the insight and guidance of our project monitor, Curtis Gilroy, Director, Special Projects and Research, USD(P&R). His comments, as well as those of his colleagues John Enns and Judy Fernandez, have been highly valuable throughout the project. We also wish to thank Jeanne Fites, Deputy Undersecretary of Defense for Requirements and Resources, for her vision and commitment to this project, and the NDRI Advisory Board for providing funding. We have benefited from the pioneering work in perstempo measurement and file development performed at the Defense Manpower Data Center, and we are, as ever, grateful for their cooperation and advice on data matters; we especially thank Robbie Brandewie, Deputy Director, Mike Dove, and Jack Leather, DMDC's expert on the perstempo file.

We owe a fundamental debt to David Gompert, Vice President of RAND's National Defense Research Institute, who initially suggested a project on the relationship between manpower and defense planning, of which this report is a product. Many colleagues at RAND provided analytical critiques of earlier versions of our work and generously offered information about policies, field experience, data, and possible effects of perstempo, all of which contributed to our knowledge and thinking. We are deeply gratified to thank Beth Asch, Glenn Gotz, Susan Hosek, Jacob Klerman, Maren Leed, Michael Mattock, Claire Levy, Michael Polich, Al Robbert, Ron Sortor, Jennifer Taw, Harry Thie, John Warner and our formal reviewers, Richard Buddin and David Chu. We received expert programming help from Janet Hanley, Rodger Madison, and Marion Oshiro at early stages of the project, and from Laurie McDonald, who computed tables on reasons why youth join the military. Finally, we are indebted to Jerry Sollinger and Ron Key for their careful work on improving the expositional clarity of the document. Any remaining errors are solely our responsibility as authors.

Chapter One

INTRODUCTION

BACKGROUND

The defense posture of the United States today recognizes a variety of threats ranging from major theater wars to smaller-scale contingencies. While threats faced by the United States have always been diverse, greater attention has been paid in the 1990s to peacetime military operations encompassing peace enforcement, peacekeeping, and humanitarian operations. At the same time, active-duty personnel have been reduced by nearly a third, and overseas stationing has been substantially reduced, especially for the Army and Air Force. Many believe that these factors—the need to be ready for major theater wars, the active involvement in diverse peacetime operations, the drawdown in force size, and the reduction in overseas basing—have combined to escalate the pace of activity in the military services. Resources are being used intensively, and the effect of the new posture and pace on readiness and personnel fosters concern.

The nature of the effect, positive or negative, is unclear, and each possibility has vigorous proponents. Those who believe the effect is negative point to several potentially significant consequences. Increased loss of trained and experienced personnel could jeopardize readiness either to wage a major theater war or to handle peacetime operations. Similarly, the loss of personnel means that the services do not derive full benefit from the dollars invested in recruiting and training and, moreover, they must spend more to replace those who leave the service before they normally would. Further, higher workloads and longer hours impose greater stress on individuals and families, reducing the quality of military life and potentially affecting readiness.[1]

---

[1] During the past few years, the Air Force, for example, has seen many of its aviators leave for jobs with the airlines. Pilots are walking away from large bonuses when they decide to leave; in 1998, the bonus was $22,000 per year for a five-year obligation, up from the $12,000 per year for a five-year obligation, up from the $12.00 per year bonus offered since 1989. "Pilots who are leaving say the top two reasons they are not taking the bonus are an increased workload—so-called 'high optemp'—and poor quality of life," with job opportunities in the airlines another major factor. (Bowman, Tom, "Pilots, Air Force feeling a crunch," *Baltimore Sun*, June 1, 1998, p. 1.)

The Army's 10th Mountain Division, based at Ft. Drum, New York, has had repeated deployments since the end of the Cold War: Somalia, the Persian Gulf, Haiti, Bosnia, Uzbekistan, Panama, the Sinai Peninsula, and relief missions following Hurricane Andrew and 1997 ice storms in the Northeast—all told, a pace that has led "most experts [to] agree that there has been a sharp drop in readiness, particularly among the so-called 'follow-on' troops that typically succeed a front-line force...." (Fritz, Mark, "A Gradual Erosion of U.S. Force," *Los Angeles Times*, November 11, 1998, pp. 1, A20.) Moreover, a recent survey of people leaving the Army "found that the biggest reason was too many deployments." (Op. cit, p. A20.)

The value of lost readiness is difficult to quantify because it depends on the nature, extent, and timing of future military contingencies. The loss of personnel from units likely to be in high demand but in short supply could create choke points affecting the capability of other units. Thus, even a loss limited to particular skills or units could have amplified negative effects. The cost of lost personnel is easier to quantify because it takes the form of increased reenlistment bonuses, increased recruiting costs, and increased training costs. More resources for personnel must come from somewhere and may reduce resources for defense R&D, procurement, and operations.

Those who argue the positive side note that being stationed abroad or deployed in a task force may be welcome experiences to many personnel who join the military not only for education, training, and career opportunity, but also for travel, adventure, and patriotism. Such experiences are likely to be more common in today's force, so their potentially positive effect on retention should be more evident. Further, in comparison to stateside basing, being deployed or based abroad may help to build skills, teamwork, flexibility, and responsiveness. In particular, units serving in peace enforcement, peacekeeping roles, and humanitarian operations may gain valuable experience that will increase their proficiency and provide lessons in leadership, combined unit operations, and logistics that will benefit units in other operations. These outcomes add to the capability to handle today's spectrum of contingencies. The experience could improve esprit d'corps and individual morale, increasing retention. Even if service abroad or operational deployment means added stress, lower morale, and lower retention in some instances, it would be expedient for the services to weigh those negatives against the gains in flexibility and operational experience.

PURPOSE AND ORGANIZATION OF STUDY

Because of this debate and its potential importance to the readiness and efficiency of the armed forces, an empirical study is required to determine whether recently increased personnel use has decreased or increased retention. We study this issue for the active-duty enlisted force, deriving measures of long or hostile duty based on the receipt of special pays, then analyze the effect of long or hostile duty on individual retention decisions. We also develop a model of deployment and retention to guide and interpret our data analysis.

The report is organized as follows. Chapter 2 presents and critiques the pay-based measures of perstempo, and Chapter 3 describes the trends in monthly perstempo rates and the extent of perstempo at the individual level. Chapter 4 introduces the theory of deployment and retention, and Chapter 5 presents results from our regression analyses and discusses various policy-relevant predictions based on the regression models. Chapter 6 contains a policy discussion of our findings. The appendices contain the full theoretical model, data on youth attitudes toward enlistment, data means and standard deviations, and regression results.

Chapter Two

PAY-BASED MEASURES OF PERSTEMPO

Personnel tempo can be measured in many dimensions. Higher tempo can mean more hours of work per day, more days per week, more weeks per year, more hours on alert, or a faster pace of work per hour. It can also mean more time on duty away from home or more time deployed, per unit of time (e.g., year). Perstempo differs from operating tempo, or optempo, but increases in optempo are generally accompanied by increases in perstempo. (Optempo is measured by sorties per day, days steaming per year, tons of cargo transported, rounds fired, fuel consumed per week, and so forth.)

MEASURING PERSTEMPO

Perstempo has increased over the past decade. More and more personnel are involved in peacetime military operations or their support, yet the process of devising standard measures has only recently begun. The Perstempo Working Group chartered by the Deputy Secretary of Defense recommended that perstempo be defined as any day away from home for operation and unit training purposes.[1] This definition captures peace operations such as Bosnia and training exercises such as the Army's at the National Training Center at Fort Irwin, California. The "day away" measure is being implemented, yet it may take a year or more before implementation is complete.

Policy makers may prefer not to wait until the various reporting systems have been modified to support the new measure. It would be useful to have credible, if incomplete, measures that offer insight into the level, trend, and effects of perstempo. Thus, for this report, we turn to existing data to construct measures bearing on two aspects of perstempo: time separated from family for 30 days or more, and duty in a hostile area or for hazardous duty. The measures are based on the receipt of special pays paid as a result of family separation or duty in an area deemed hostile, namely, Family Separation Allowance (FSA) and Hostile Fire Pay (HFP). The amount and conditions for receipt of these pays are common across the services, and therefore measures based on the pays are comparable, although the operations, missions, and activities giving rise to these pays may differ.

---

[1]U.S. Department of Defense, Report of the PERSTEMPO Working Group, Washington, D.C.: U.S. Department of Defense, July 12, 1996.

We recognize that these measures will miss much of what qualifies as perstempo under the DoD definition of a "day away." We also recognize that pay-based measures have limitations of their own that we discuss below. However, because they relate to pay, individual service members and the services themselves are motivated to ensure the accuracy of these measures. Also, the pay-based measures can signal whether duty was hostile, and it is not yet clear if the "day away" measure will make that distinction. Thus, even when the new measure is ready, pay-based measures may be a valuable complement.

Personnel who are separated from their family members for at least 30 days receive FSA. The period begins on the day of deployment, and, once 30 consecutive days away have passed, individuals are eligible to receive the allowance. It is paid to personnel stationed abroad on unaccompanied tours, afloat, or deployed in military operations, in each case for 30 days or more. The purpose of FSA is:

> ... to partially reimburse, on average, members of the uniformed services involuntarily separated from their dependents for the reasonable amount of extra expenses that result from such separation, and to reimburse members who must maintain a residence in the United States for their dependents and another home overseas for themselves for the average expenses of maintaining the overseas home.[2]

FSA for service members involuntarily separated from their families is referred to as FSA Type II, while FSA for service members who must maintain a second home overseas because bachelor quarters are not available is referred to as FSA Type I. We use both types. FSA II was increased from $30 per month to $60 per month in 1985 and $75 per month in 1991. FSA I is equal to the monthly Basic Allowance for Quarters (BAQ) without dependents.

The purpose of Hostile Fire Pay is:

> To provide an additional payment during periods of nominal peace to personnel subject to hostile fire or to explosion of hostile mines; to personnel serving in hostile fire areas or on vessels or aircraft, or in units, that engage in hostile action, whether in a designated hostile fire area or not; and to personnel on duty in foreign areas in which they are subject to the threat of physical harm or imminent danger because of civil insurrection, civil war, terrorism, or wartime conditions.[3]

For brevity, we refer to HFP as being paid for duty in areas deemed hostile. This would include, for example, air crews flying missions into hostile areas though not necessarily based in those areas, Army units serving in hostile areas, and Navy and Marine Corps personnel on ships deployed to hostile waters. As of 1996, near the time of our reenlistment analysis (Chapter 4), the following were designated HFP areas: Cambodia, Iran, Lebanon, El Salvador, Columbia, Peru, Sudan, Afghanistan, Laos, Kuwait, Liberia, Iraq, the Persian Gulf, Saudi Arabia, Yemen, Turkey, Angola, Chad, Mozambique, Slovenia, Croatia, Bosnia-Herzegovina and the remaining land

---

[2]DoD, 1996, p. 773.

[3]Ibid., p. 173.

area within the former country of Yugoslavia, Somalia, and Haiti.[4] Clearly, HFP carries a judgmental component of what is or is not hostile duty, and a country's hostile-duty designation can change. We assume the change reflects a change in the actual risk of hazardous duty. Further, some missions to nonhostile areas may also involve hazards, i.e., the hostile duty designation does not encompass all duty with hazards.

The level of HFP has been $150 per month since mid-1990.[5] HFP does not require personnel to have dependents and does not require a minimum time of service such as 30 days. HFP, also known as Hazardous Duty Pay, has recently been renamed and is now called Imminent Danger Pay (IDP). Because our data cover the period before the name change, we use the former.

Recapping the information on pay levels, FSA II adds $75 per month to a service member's pay, and HFP adds $150 per month; the two together add $225. Examples of personnel receiving FSA only are those with dependents who are stationed abroad on unaccompanied tours, on unaccompanied stateside training, or on unaccompanied exercises or cruises lasting 30 days or longer. All personnel with duty in a hostile area would receive HFP, and if that duty lasts 30 days or longer, those personnel with dependents would also receive FSA if they were not already doing so. For instance, personnel coming from the United States, where they were based with their families, would begin drawing FSA when on duty in a hostile area for 30 days or more, whereas personnel coming from an unaccompanied tour (e.g., the Army in Korea) would already be drawing FSA.

To place these amounts in perspective, we refer to basic pay levels for the first-term and early-career ranks of E-3, E-4, E-5, and E-6. The 1996 basic pay was $1074.90 per month for an E-3 with over two years of service, $1209.30 for an E-4 with over three years of service, $1380.90 for an E-5 with over four years of service, $1471.80 for an E-5 with over six years of service, and $1680.90 for an E-6 with over eight years of service. To illustrate, HFP is $150/$1209.30 or 12.4 percent of a junior E-4's basic pay, and HFP plus FSA is ($150 + $75)/$1471.80 or 15.3 percent of an E-5's basic pay.

In practice, several factors reduce this percentage. Some personnel receive bonuses or special pays (e.g., flight pay, sea pay, sub pay), which add to monthly take-home pay. Further, the amount of FSA or HFP *per year* will depend on the number of

---

[4]Beginning March 1, 1998, the following are designated imminent danger pay areas: Afghanistan, Albania, Algeria, Angola, Arabian Gulf, Azerbaijan, Bahrain, Bosnia-Herzegovina, Burundi, Cambodia, Colombia, Croatia, Egypt, El Salvador, Georgia, Greece, Haiti, Iran, Iraq, Jordan, Kuwait, Lebanon, Liberia, Macedonia, Montenegro, Pakistan, Peru, Qatar, Rwanda, Saudi Arabia, Serbia, Sierra Leone, Somalia, Sudan, Tajikistan, Turkey, and Zaire. In each case the designation applies to all or a designated part of the land area, and in some cases also applies to the airspace. (Compart, 1998, p. 8.)

[5]The 1986 Authorization Act, Public Law 99-145, reestablished the linkage between hostile fire pay and hazardous duty incentive pay originally established by the Uniformed Services Pay Act of 1963. Hazardous duties include such as parachute jumping and explosive demolition. The 1986 Act equated HFP to the lowest rate of pay for hazardous duty. HFP was $65 per month from September 1, 1965, until the enactment of the 1986 Authorization Act in 1985, at which time it increased to $110 per month. It was temporarily increased to $150 per month on August 1, 1990, in conjunction with the Gulf War, and subsequent legislation made this level permanent. In addition, Public Law 102-190 (1991) repealed the prohibition on payment of hostile fire or imminent danger pay during time of war declared by Congress. (Ibid., pp. 173–181.)

months separated or deployed to a hostile area; shorter separations and deployments make FSA and HFP a smaller portion of annual earnings. Finally, many personnel are single and have no other dependents, and therefore are not eligible for FSA. Others marry during the year and become eligible.

FSA and HFP can be used to create various measures of perstempo. We use the measures to describe the extent of long or hostile duty and analyze its impact on enlisted retention.

SPECIFIC MEASURES

We present four measures of perstempo. Three of them are new, and the other was developed previously by the Defense Manpower Data Center (DMDC). The first measure provides an aggregate estimate of personnel involved in long or hostile duty in a given month, where "long" means 30 days or more and "hostile" means duty in an area deemed hostile. The second measure, developed by the DMDC, indicates personnel whose unit had long or hostile duty, i.e., the unit was "separated/deployed." The first measure includes separation or deployment with one's unit, or separation or deployment as an individual (usually attached to another unit). The second measure emphasizes only separation or deployment with one's unit. The difference is important because the Army, Air Force, and Marine Corps often construct deploying task forces by augmenting units with individuals drawn from other units; thus, individuals may be separated or deployed even though their unit is not. We call the first measure *long or hostile duty—total* and the second measure *long or hostile duty—unit.* The second measure is in principle a subset of the first measure.[6] We use these aggregate measures to estimate the fraction of the force on long or hostile duty in a month.

By comparison, the third and fourth measures concern the amount of such duty over an extended period. These measures are *months* and *episodes* of long or hostile duty over a 24-month period.

The DMDC Perstempo File, our data base, contains longitudinal observations on service members in, or entering, active-duty service over the period from December 1987 through June 1996. The data cover the last month in each quarter from December 1987 to December 1992 and each month from January 1993 to June 1996.

Long or Hostile Duty—Total

We construct the long or hostile duty—total by first recognizing that personnel with dependents can potentially receive both FSA and HFP, and we therefore have full information on whether they had a long separation (FSA is received), hostile duty

---

[6]Exceptions may apply. The DMDC unit separated/deployed indicator is attached to *all* members of a unit, but some members may be ill, injured, in a disciplinary status, or in training and thus do not separate or deploy with their unit. Based on our data, we believe this over-imputation occurs only 1–2 percent of the time.

Table 2.1

**Measures of Long or Hostile Duty Based on
Family Separation Allowance (FSA) and
Hostile Fire Pay (HFP)**

Hostile Fire Pay	Family Separation Allowance	
	No	Yes
No	None	Long (≥ 30 days)
Yes	Hostile	Long and hostile

(HFP is received), or both. Table 2.1 illustrates this. We then use certain information from personnel with dependents to help estimate long duty for personnel without dependents, for whom the presence or absence of hostile duty is known.

Personnel without dependents are eligible for HFP but not FSA. Because of this, we cannot use FSA to determine the percentage of these personnel who have long separation/deployment. However, if we assume that personnel without dependents are as likely to have long duty as their counterparts with dependents, we can overcome this limitation.[7] Moreover, we can incorporate the information we have on personnel without dependents, namely, whether they received HFP. Our procedure is to divide personnel without dependents into two groups depending on whether they received HFP, and for each group impute the percentage with long separation/deployment based on that percentage for personnel with dependents and receiving, or not receiving, HFP. We condition on HFP because this information is available for personnel without dependents; our estimates should therefore be more precise by incorporating it than by assuming that personnel without dependents—regardless of HFP—have the same pattern as personnel with dependents. Also, we emphasize that the imputation is done for a group, not for individuals.[8] Further, because the imputation is based on a credible assumption, the results should be accurate.

We perform the imputation by service, month in quarter, first term/early career (defined below), and one-digit primary occupational specialty. For example, the chance of long separation may (and does) vary by occupational specialty, and the procedure is sensitive to this by means of the occupation groupings.

Having imputed, we can now infer long or hostile perstempo for all members of the group, whether with or without dependents. This allows us to create *total* counts of long or hostile duty, i.e., aggregate estimates of the number of personnel whose perstempo in a given month was long, hostile, both, or neither.

---

[7]This assumption is quite reasonable because only a small fraction of personnel—those married to another service member—are apt to have separation or deployment conditioned on their dependents' status.

[8]If the method were applied to individuals, some *percent* of the month would be assumed a long separation/deployment, conditional on whether HFP was received. We follow a different imputation procedure for individuals, described in creating the months measure.

Long or Hostile Duty—Unit

The second measure, long or hostile duty—unit, assigns each service member a flag indicating whether the service member's unit was separated/deployed in a given month. The procedure for creating the unit separated/deployed indicator, developed by the DMDC, works from the individual up to the unit and then back to the individual. Individual records contain a unit identification code (UIC), and for each UIC a program keeps count of the number of unit members, the number with family members, and the number with FSA or HFP receipt. If the unit contains at least 10 members, at least 30 percent of the unit members have dependents, and at least 60 percent of those with dependents receive FSA or HFP, the unit is deemed separated/deployed in the month. If so, the separated/deployed flag is turned on for each unit member. If fewer than 30 percent of unit members have dependents, the flag is not turned on; if more than 30 percent have dependents but fewer than 60 percent of those members have FSA or HFP, the flag is not turned on. With its hurdle of 60 percent FSA or HFP recipiency, the measure seems well targeted to identify unit separation/deployment as opposed to individual separation or deployment. We therefore use it as the basis of our long or hostile duty—unit measure.

We also use the unit deployed/separated flag in constructing the months and episodes measures, described next.

Months: Total and Hostile

We have created two measures of the individual's perstempo over a longer period of time. The first is total months over a 24-month window either separated *for at least 30 days* consecutively or deployed to a hostile area. (Again, temporary duty of less than 30 days is omitted from the data.) The second measure is hostile months, i.e., the number of months within 24 months in which one was deployed to a hostile area. The first measure captures any long separation or hostile duty, while the second is limited to hostile duty. Further, the difference between total months and hostile months equals months of long, nonhostile duty. These measures reveal the *individual's* cumulative experience and therefore complement the monthly measures that show the fraction of personnel in a month who have long or hostile duty.

To construct total months and hostile months we exploited the longitudinal nature of the perstempo data. The data contain monthly information on FSA and HFP receipt from January 1993 to June 1996 but only one monthly observation per quarter for December 1987 to December 1992. Because continual monthly observations are lacking before January 1993, we based the measures on the period from January 1993 onward to June 1996. As data accumulate in coming years, it will be possible to compute these measures on an ongoing basis.

Because we are interested in the effect of perstempo on retention, we have computed total and hostile months only for personnel facing a reenlistment decision. We selected personnel with 10 years of service or fewer and having an expiration of term of service (ETS) date during July 1995–June 1996. We then identified the actual date of the stay/leave decision.

Most personnel who leave the service stay until their ETS date; some depart earlier under early-out programs. Most who stay make that decision several months before the ETS date. Deciding early allows them to capitalize on training opportunities, opportunities for assignments to certain locations, or existing bonus levels (known with certainty, versus uncertain future bonus levels). It may also enable them to accompany their unit or another unit on a deployment or foreign stationing that, with a short enlistment time remaining, they otherwise would not be able to do.

The timing of this decision raises the possibility that a retention decision may enable a desired deployment or separation, or alternatively, that a prospective deployment could have an adverse effect on retention. Our objective is to analyze the effect of perstempo on reenlistment; thus, we are interested in causality from deployment or separation to retention. To avoid reverse causality, we count back six months from the date of decision. (We assume six months is long enough because most separations or deployments are three to six months long.) We then count back over 24 months to tabulate the number of months separated or deployed. Although a longer period might be better, we had to use 24 months because monthly observations are not available prior to January 1993. The 24-month window applies to everyone in the sample and ensures a constant period of exposure. However, because the 24 months are not the exact same months for everyone, even though they are all circa 1993–1995, there may be slight differences in the actual exposure to perstempo.

The longitudinal record of long separation or hostile deployment is complete for personnel with family members throughout the 24-month window because they are eligible to receive FSA and HFP in every month. The record is incomplete for personnel without family members in some or all of the 24 months, however, because FSA cannot be received in those months. As a result, information on hostile duty in a given month is available for everyone, and information on long separation is available only for personnel with dependents. This is a serious limitation because many personnel, especially junior personnel, do not have families. Moreover, personnel with dependents at the end of the observation period may not have them at the beginning; many personnel marry between ages 18 and 30.

We therefore again sought an approach to fill the missing data gap for personnel without dependents, or more precisely, for the months in the 24-month window in which a service member had no dependents. We chose to use the DMDC unit separated/deployed indicator. Thus, for a person without dependents in a given month, we first checked if HFP was received and, if so, we used HFP in building measures of total and hostile months. If not, we used unit separated/deployed. Specifically, if the individual received HFP, we treated the month as hostile. If the individual did not receive HFP but the unit was separated/deployed, we treated the month as a long-separation, nonhostile month. That is, the DMDC indicator allowed us to impute long, nonhostile months. Calling these months nonhostile is accurate only from the *individual's* perspective. Other members of the unit might have had hostile duty that month.

Although this approach closes a significant portion of the data gap, it still under-counts nonhostile months, as discussed below. (There is no undercount of hostile months because they are indicated by HFP.)

At the same time, it suggests an additional measure for our empirical analysis, namely, months separated/deployed *with one's unit.* The measure is created strictly by means of the DMDC unit separated/deployed indicator applied in all months whether dependents were present or not. The unit indicator gives us a measure of months (and episodes) of a unit's long or hostile perstempo. Such perstempo might include, for example, being stationed in Korea[9] or Okinawa, 30-day or longer unit training or exercises, humanitarian assistance missions, nation building, e.g., build-ing a road in Guatemala, and peacekeeping/peace enforcement deployments.[10]

Episodes: Total and Hostile

Episodes are another measure of the cumulative extent of an *individual's* long or hostile perstempo. An episode is a consecutive run of months during which an indicator of long separation or hostile duty is on. We include partial episodes, i.e., those occurring at the beginning or end of the 24-month window, as well as whole episodes occurring within the window. Like the months measures, we have total episodes, based on long separation or hostile duty, and hostile episodes, which are episodes containing at least one month of hostile duty. This is a liberal definition of hostile episode. It includes, for example, predeployment training at a training site, transit time, duty in a hostile area, and return home.

CRITIQUE OF MEASURES

While the perstempo measures should provide reasonably accurate information about important aspects of perstempo, several shortcomings should be remembered.

- The measures miss short, nonhostile separation or deployment. This is especially unfortunate for the Air Force, which, like the other services, is actively involved in peacetime operations. Many Air Force operational missions do not require a month's separation and do not occur within hostile countries or hostile

---

[9]Korea is an unaccompanied tour for the Army. As a result, personnel with dependents receive FSA, so the unit deployment indicator will indicate that the unit is deployed. Therefore, this deployment can be imputed to personnel without dependents. In contrast, Germany is an accompanied tour. As a result, personnel with dependents do not receive FSA, the unit deployment indicator does not indicate deploy-ment, and no imputation of deployment can be made to personnel without dependents. In effect, accom-panied tours such as Germany are treated as though the unit were based in the United States. Yet for personnel without dependents, being stationed in Germany may have many similarities with being stationed in Korea: away from the United States and from stateside friends. This disparity in the apparent long, nonhostile perstempo of personnel without dependents is clearly the product of tracking perstempo via pay measures rather than basing and mission information.

[10]Further, because HFP can be used to identify a person's hostile months (and episodes), we can also at-tempt to separate the effect of hostile months from the effect of unit separation/deployment in our re-gression analysis of reenlistment. Controlling for hostile months, unit deployment will convey the impact of long nonhostile unit deployments on reenlistment.

airspace, and the measures miss these activities. This shortcoming applies to the other services as well, though probably not to the same degree.

- The long or hostile duty—unit measure undercounts when the unit is separated or deployed and contains 10 or more members, but fewer than 30 percent of the unit members have families. This particularly affects the Marine Corps, where a high proportion of personnel are in their first term and unmarried, making it more likely that an entire unit will not meet the 30-percent threshold. However, the threshold can be seen as a constructive compromise, low enough to include most units yet high enough to provide a sufficient sample to assure that exceeding the 60-percent FSA/HFP criterion is statistically meaningful. Thus, the measure is relatively accurate for the Army, Navy, and Air Force, though it most likely undercounts unit perstempo in the Marine Corps.

- The measures do not provide information about the pace of work or the conditions and dangers associated with separation or deployment. The services and OSD recognize these shortcomings, and the development of new measures can be expected to mitigate or overcome them.

- Use of the DMDC unit separated/deployed indicator to impute *long, nonhostile* perstempo to personnel without dependents undercounts such experiences.[11] (Hostile perstempo is not undercounted because the indicator of hostile perstempo, Hostile Fire Pay, is available for all service members whether or not they have dependents.) The undercount of long, nonhostile months occurs not because of any problem with the DMDC indicator, but because there are *nonunit* separations and deployments. To gauge the extent of undercount, we have used personnel with dependents, a group for whom we have full information, and employed the DMDC indicator to impute long, nonhostile months to them in those months when they did not receive HFP. Because we have full information, we can use their long, nonhostile months as a standard of comparison for imputed long, nonhostile months.

Table 2.2 shows the percentage difference between imputed and actual long, nonhostile months. The percent shortfall ranges from 19 percent to 68 percent. For instance, imputed months for Air Force early-career personnel were 52 percent of actual months.

Table 2.2

Percent Undercount of Long, Nonhostile Months

	Army	Air Force	Navy	Marine Corps
First term	44	65	24	64
Early career	41	52	19	68

---

[11]The emphasis here is on *nonhostile* months because all personnel, whether with or without dependents, can receive HFP; we therefore have an indicator for hostile months.

Generally, the extent of a person's undercount of long, nonhostile months depends on his or her dependents status. Persons with dependents over the entire 24-month window have no undercount, persons without dependents over the full window have an undercount on average as shown in Table 2.2, and persons with dependents for some months have an undercount reduced proportionately. In particular, the undercount will be less for early-career personnel than for first-term personnel because more early careerists are married. (Because they are married, they are eligible for FSA; we have no need to impute long, nonhostile months.) This observation is true for all services, yet especially relevant to the Marine Corps. We noted above that because of the low marriage rate in the Marine Corps, unit separation/deployment will be undercounted, and now we recognize that higher married rates among early-career personnel help offset the undercount. That is, because more early careerists are married, we have less need to impute; therefore, the count of long, nonhostile months will be relatively more accurate among early-career personnel.

In sum, we expect long, nonhostile months to be undercounted; the undercount will be less for early-career than first-term personnel, and if a trouble spot remains, it is among first-term Marines. We bear these data limitations in mind when discussing the regression results (Chapter 5).

That said, the *meaning* of the undercount is less obvious. For all personnel, with or without dependents, we can rely on the DMDC unit-separated/deployed indicator to reflect separation/deployment with one's unit.[12] Therefore, the undercounted long, nonhostile months probably reflect mostly *individual* temporary duty. This could involve activities including military education (e.g., before promotion to E-5 Army soldiers must complete a Primary Leadership Development Course that can be as long as 30 days) and detachment to other units, for instance. A common feature of the undercount is being away from home base and away from one's unit, but other aspects of these deployments could be quite diverse. Consequently, the effect of unit deployment on reenlistment might be different than the effect of non-unit deployment, i.e., the portion for which we have an undercount. By using the DMDC unit separated/deployed indicator, we can build measures of *unit deployment over a 24-month period* and analyze the effect on reenlistment. Unit deployment is a subset of an individual's total perstempo experience, the primary focus of our analysis, and we report the results as a data exploration at the end of the next chapter.

Another consideration is less quantifiable. Although we have measures of long or hostile duty, the context of these measures differs by service because of how the services are equipped and operated. The Navy staffs ships and maintains a permanent presence in forward areas (sometimes intermittently) by rotating like types of ships through operational areas. The operating cycle, about five years, is largely driven by the need for major overhaul of ships. Ships complete an overhaul and begin to prepare for a deployment of six months. About three such deployments will occur over the five-year cycle, interspersed with shorter-duration cruises from home port for training, short exercises, and so forth. The Navy attempts to match its as-

---

[12]We should not forget that unit separated/deployed is undercounted for the Marine Corps.

signments to the five-year cycle, but exceptions occur. A sailor assigned to a carrier for a full five-year cycle can expect to spend less than half that period away from home with no single separation lasting longer than six months. The Navy continues this operational style begun during the Cold War. Overseas deployments, as part of today's various contingency operations, fit this scheme reasonably well, with few readiness costs because the activities tend to be complementary. (Haiti has been the only deployment that could not be accommodated during normal deployment cycles.) Naval aviation squadrons also follow this pattern of working up to a deployment, even though they rotate on and off ships.

The Army operates quite differently. It permanently stations large units and rotates small units through them. Thus, while the large unit remains in place, its personnel change, generally on a three-year cycle. Exceptions occur for hardship areas such as Korea, where a normal tour is one year.

Even though the ground-combat units of the Marine Corps resemble those of the Army in organization and equipment, they operate differently. The Marine Corps rotates its units through a cycle much the way the Navy rotates crews for its ships. Thus, it also uses a preparation-deployment-recovery cycle, although the length differs from that of the Navy. The Marines prepare for 90 days, deploy for 180 days, and recover for 90 days before beginning the cycle again. The personnel-assignment pattern supports four such cycles; that is, people serve four-year tours.

The Air Force also is different. It deploys units, such as squadrons, but it does not operate them as collective units. Rather, it employs whatever number of weapon systems are needed, usually in conjunction with other types of aircraft. Because the Air Force employs a tailored set of aircraft for each mission, operational flexibility across the entire unit is a key concern.

Thus, people join the services with different expectations conditioned by the service's operating procedures. For example, people who join the Navy generally expect to go to sea unless they enlist for a specific land-based skill, and they understand that sea duty typically lasts several months. So someone enlisting in the Navy would have very different expectations from, for example, someone enlisting in the Air Force, who might expect some short deployments but would anticipate serving primarily at an Air Force base. Thus, relative to expectations, the effect of three six-month deployments over a four-year enlistment would be different depending on the service, and could have different effects on retention.

Chapter Three

LONG OR HOSTILE DUTY TRENDS AND EXTENT

We review the trend and extent of perstempo by a variety of different measures. We describe monthly rates over 1987–1996, distinguishing changes in hostile and non-hostile duty. We further describe individual incidence, months, and episodes over a 24-month period circa 1993–1995. By presenting information on long or hostile duty trends and extent among personnel, we establish a context in which to place the regression analysis of the next chapter.

It is commonly asserted in the defense community that the pace of perstempo began increasing around 1990, first with the noticeable spike in activity required by Desert Shield and Desert Storm, and subsequently because of a variety of peacetime operations including Haiti, Somalia, and Bosnia. We find that the trends in long or hostile duty differ by service, with a smaller relative increase in overall rates for the Navy and Marine Corps, given their higher initial rates, and relatively large increases for the Army and Air Force, which had much lower initial rates. Also, the increases reflect a shift toward more hostile duty.

The trends in monthly rates carry through to the occupational level. The correspondence between the overall and occupational rates is especially strong for the Navy and Marine Corps, where much perstempo takes the form of unit separation/deployment. Army and Air Force occupations also have a strong correspondence with overall perstempo, but greater variation occurs—probably because of the Army's practice of attaching individuals to deploying task forces and the Air Force's varied missions and aircraft requirements.

We find a large difference between the total rate and unit rate for the Army and Air Force. Focusing on the unit rate would underestimate the overall rate by a factor of two over much of our period of observation, 1987–1996. Total and unit rates are similar for the Navy. The underestimate of the Marine Corps unit rate, however, exaggerates the difference between the Corps' total and unit rates.

Shifting from these monthly rates, we observe a far higher incidence of perstempo over 24 months. Whereas monthly rates in the post–Gulf War period averaged 8–10 percent for the Army, 6–7 percent for the Air Force, 11–12 percent for the Navy, and 14–15 percent for the Marine Corps, the incidence of long or hostile duty over 24 months was around 40 percent in the Army, 30 percent in the Air Force, 70 percent and 40 percent among Navy first-term and early-career personnel, respectively, and 50 percent in the Marine Corps. Moreover, there were marked differences at the occupational level, much more so than for the monthly rates. On average, the 24-month rates translated into 3–4 months separated/deployed for the Army and Air Force, a bit higher for the Marine Corps, and 5–7 months for the Navy. Most commonly, long or hostile duty occurred in a single episode, yet many personnel experienced two episodes and some had three or more. Finally, a substantial fraction, one-third to two-thirds, of these episodes were hostile, i.e., required duty in a hostile area.

TRENDS IN LONG OR HOSTILE DUTY—TOTAL

In 1987, the active-duty forces stood at 2.1 million personnel: 1.8 million enlisted and 0.3 million officers. By 1996, the strength had been reduced to 1.4 million personnel, with enlisted and officers taking proportionate cuts. Also by 1996, the Cold War had ended, the Gulf War had been fought, and strategic attention was shifting away from an emphasis on readiness for a superpower confrontation. The U.S. national security posture continued to require, as it had for many years, a capacity for large- and small-scale contingencies, though there appeared to be greater emphasis on the capacity to handle peace operations including peace enforcement, peacekeeping, and humanitarian assistance. The posture also required, as it had previously, a capacity for disaster relief, drug interdiction, show of force, nation building, and steps to strengthen relations with strategic partners. The increased emphasis on peace enforcement, peacekeeping, and humanitarian assistance meant changes in peacetime optempo and perstempo. As mentioned, our measures of perstempo, while missing some aspects, capture changes linked to long separations and deployments to hostile areas.

By Service

Figures 3.1–3.4 show total rates for long or hostile duty by service. The rates automatically adjust for the scale effect of the drawdown in military personnel. Each figure depicts the long, nonhostile rate (top), the hostile rate (middle), and the total rate (bottom). (Note that the figures have different scales.)

The Army's total rate (Figure 3.1 bottom) has increased, from 6 percent before the Gulf War and before the end of the Cold War to a higher and more volatile range. This increase results from higher long, nonhostile perstempo (Figure 3.1 top) and higher hostile perstempo (middle). The percentage of personnel with long, nonhostile perstempo has risen from 6 percent to 8 percent. This is consistent with the decline in Army strength being accompanied by a not-quite-proportionate decline in the number of personnel stationed abroad on unaccompanied tours. Probably the majority of these tours were to Korea. The Army treats Korea as a "short tour" (one year in length and unaccompanied), whereas Europe is a "long tour" (three years in length and accompanied).

Army hostile duty (Figure 3.1 middle) is portrayed as the sum of short (less than 30 days) and long (30 or more days) deployments. Short deployments are the gray

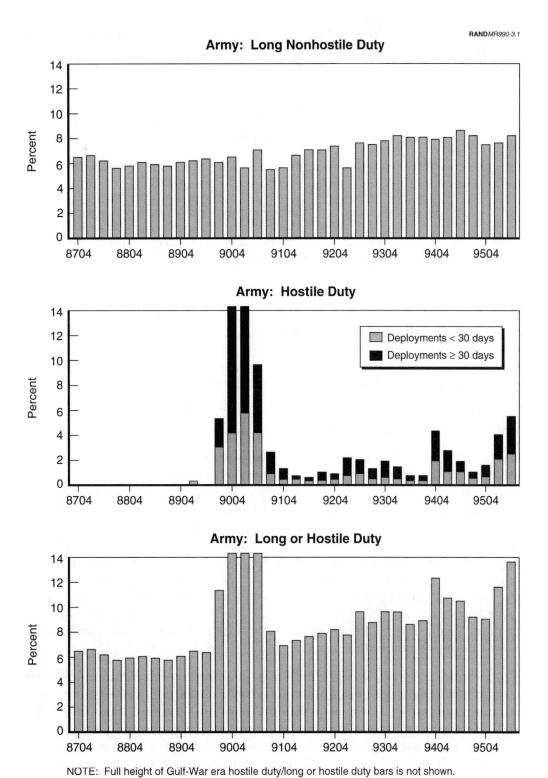

NOTE: Full height of Gulf-War era hostile duty/long or hostile duty bars is not shown.

Figure 3.1—Percentage of Army Enlisted Personnel with Long Nonhostile,
Hostile, and Long or Hostile Duty

portion of the bar, and long deployments are the black. The Gulf War accounts for the spike beginning in the third quarter of 1990 and ending a year later in the third quarter of 1991. (The full height of these spikes is not shown.) Yet since then the Army has had 1–5 percent of its troops on hostile duty in any month. Five percent occurs at the end of the data series and heralds a growing involvement in Bosnia. Since the commitment of troops to Bosnia has continued into 1998, the percentage of troops deployed to a hostile area has probably remained relatively high.

This level of activity can have important repercussions within the Army, as the *Army Times* notes:

> The high tempo of operations is . . . stretching Army resources to the breaking point. In addition to keeping 6,800 troops in Bosnia during 1997, supported by an additional 3,700 troops in Hungary and Croatia, the Army kept a battalion deployed in Macedonia, another in the Sinai and a third in Panama. U.S. Army Europe units are also frequently tapped to send small elements to East European countries on Partnership for Peace exercises. (Naylor, 1998, p. 18.)

The article further comments that because so much time is required to prepare for and recover from these peacekeeping deployments, some commanders and NCOs in Europe complain that they have little time left to train units for their primary mission of maneuver warfare. Others believe the Bosnia deployment builds teamwork, creates camaraderie, and allows units to practice wartime tasks.

For the Air Force, our measures show a doubling of long or hostile duty from the late 1980s to the 1990s (Figure 3.2). The increase is due to hostile duty.

Setting aside the Gulf War, the figure shows a striking contrast between the late 1980s, when virtually no hostile duty occurred, and the 1990s, where hostile duty accounts for half the total rate. Further, during the post–Gulf War 1990s, the mix of hostile duty has changed from 50 percent short separations to around 90 percent. This may represent a gradual withdrawal of resources from the Gulf region, e.g., aircraft based in Saudi Arabia, and an increase in the number of missions flown from "safe" bases into hostile territory. Also, the Air Force shows a smaller Gulf-War spike than the other services. However, many Air Force missions originated at bases elsewhere, especially Europe, and only the flight crews, but not the ground crews at those bases, were eligible to receive Hostile Fire Pay. Aircraft are often forward deployed, and personnel (air crews) rotate forward and back. (Additionally, many flight-crew members are officers and not included in this report.)

Although the Air Force's long or hostile duty rates are lower than that of the other services, this should not be taken as an indication that such duty has not increased at least as much for the Air Force as the other services. The Air Force's lower rate reflects how the Air Force is organized and based. A large ground support team is required to keep the aircraft mission-ready, and, understandably, aircraft bases are predominately located in nonhostile areas. This also points to how interservice differences can affect the measured rates. In the Navy, some aircraft support teams would be onboard ship, and if the ship were deployed to a hostile area the team members would be counted in the rates.

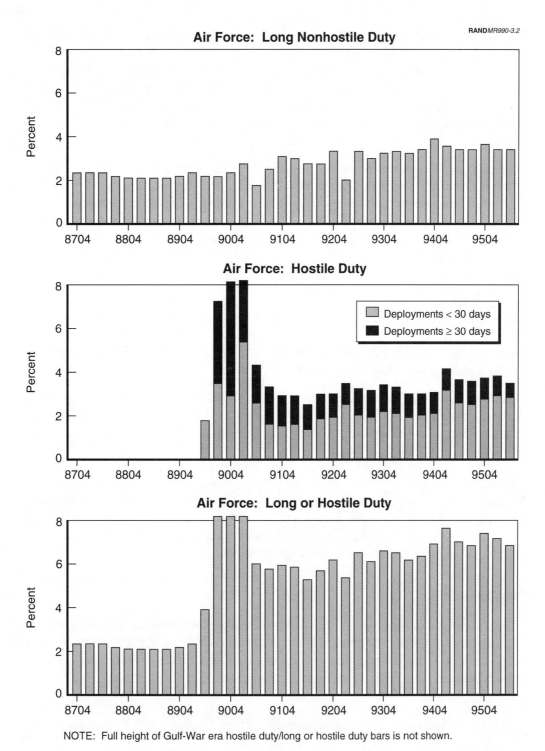

RAND*MR990-3.2*

NOTE: Full height of Gulf-War era hostile duty/long or hostile duty bars is not shown.

Figure 3.2—Percentage of Air Force Enlisted Personnel with Long Nonhostile, Hostile,
and Long or Hostile Duty

In related research on the pace of peacetime activities in the Air Force, Fossen et al. (1997) found that in the mid-1990s many personnel at home base reported long, stressful weeks. The pace and pressure arose from several factors, including a challenging schedule of inspections and exercises and the extra effort required by the increase in peacetime operations involving hostile duty (Figure 3.2 middle). The Air Force has recognized the problem and is implementing reductions in workload and pace.

Long or hostile duty trends for the Navy and Marine Corps should be viewed in tandem (Figures 3.3 and 3.4). This is because Marine Corps units often sail with the Navy, and as a result the services have similar tempos. The Marines are also called upon to participate in ground actions, perhaps the most prominent recent action being Somalia. Involvement in such actions causes the Marine Corps rates to be higher than the Navy's. (The apparent drop in Marine Corps rates from the second quarter of 1991 to the second quarter of 1992 has been identified by DMDC as underreporting and should be ignored.)

Overall Navy perstempo (Figure 3.3 bottom) rose by about 3 percent in the post–Gulf War years versus the prewar years. In the postwar years the Navy averaged 13.4 percent and the Marine Corps 17.8 percent. This compares with post–Gulf War levels of 9.1 percent for the Army and 6.3 percent for the Air Force.

Both the Navy and Marine Corps have experienced increases in the proportion of hostile perstempo. Set against a fairly constant nonhostile rate, this change suggests that the Navy has reduced its nonhostile operations in proportion to its size, maintained its afloat/ashore rotation policy, and now its personnel spend more time under way in hostile waters. The rotation policy calls for a maximum of six months under way spelled by twice as much time in home port. The home-port time includes time either ashore or under way, but not deployed.[1] The underway-but-not-deployed category includes time spent on short cruises following maintenance activities, with onboard refresher training, and typically does not involve separations of 30 days or longer or steaming into hostile waters.

By Occupation

Table 3.1 displays total rates by occupational group before and after the Gulf War.[2] By focusing on the occupation level, Table 3.1 disentangles occupation changes from changes in the mix of occupations, both of which contribute to total rates. We find that total rates rose in all occupations in all services.

---

[1]The Navy also has "a requirement that each unit spend at least 50 percent of its time in home port during the most recent 5-year period." (Cooke et al., 1992, p. 1, who cite OPNAV Instruction 3000.13, *Personnel Tempo of Operations*, OP-642C2, February 7, 1990.)

[2]Again, this is the monthly rate of long or hostile duty. The prewar period runs from the fourth quarter of 1987 to the second quarter of 1990, and the postwar period covers the second quarter of 1992 to the second quarter of 1996. Cell entries show the average monthly rates for the prewar and postwar periods, respectively, and the average is based on the last month of the quarter, as in Figures 3.1–3.4.

RAND*MR990-3.3*

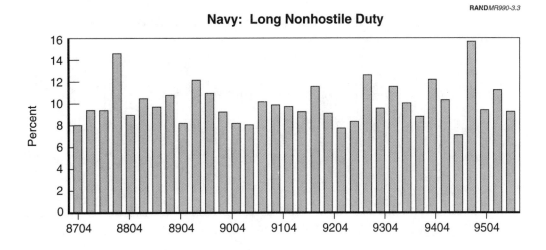

Navy: Long Nonhostile Duty

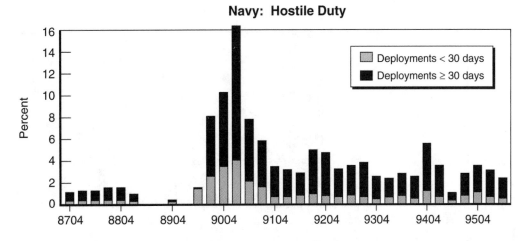

Navy: Hostile Duty

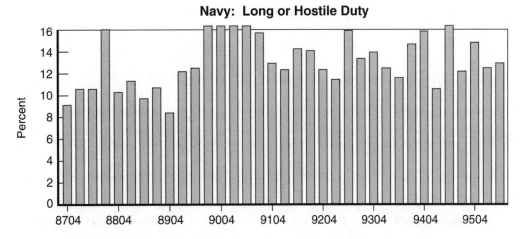

Navy: Long or Hostile Duty

NOTE: Full height of Gulf-War era hostile duty/long or hostile duty bars is not shown.

Figure 3.3—Percentage of Navy Enlisted Personnel with Long Nonhostile, Hostile, and Long or Hostile Duty

RAND*MR990-3.4*

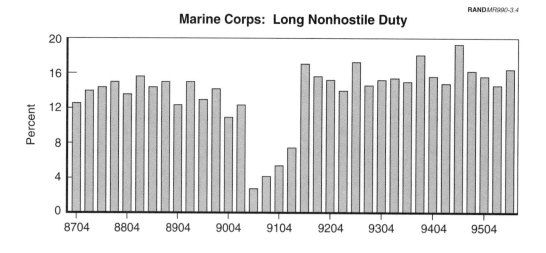

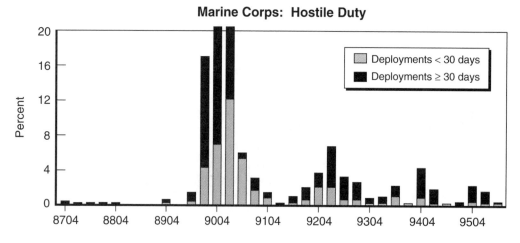

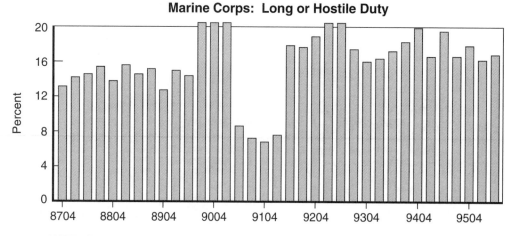

NOTE: Full height of Gulf-War era hostile duty/long or hostile duty bars is not shown.

Figure 3.4—Percentage of Marine Corps Enlisted Personnel with Long Nonhostile, Hostile, and Long or Hostile Duty

Table 3.1

Total Rates by Occupation Before and After the Gulf War
(percentages)

	Army		Air Force		Navy		Marines	
Occupation	Prewar	Post-war	Prewar	Post-war	Prewar	Post-war	Prewar	Post-war
Infantry, gun crews, and seamanship	6.2	9.2	2.4	9.1	13.6	16.2	19.8	25.2
Electronic equipment repairers	6.8	10.0	2.1	5.9	9.6	13.0	10.5	13.3
Communications and intelligence	6.6	9.4	2.9	5.9	11.2	14.0	14.5	17.4
Medical and dental specialists	4.0	7.1	1.3	3.0	4.7	5.8	NA	NA
Other technical and allied specialists	5.7	7.8	2.9	6.0	7.3	9.2	8.1	10.1
Functional support and administration	5.0	7.8	2.3	5.4	9.1	11.9	9.1	11.6
Electrical/mechanical equipment repairers	7.1	11.0	2.0	7.3	11.9	14.2	12.9	16.6
Craftsmen	6.8	9.5	2.9	6.8	14.2	16.3	13.6	17.2
Service and supply handlers	6.3	9.8	2.8	7.1	12.7	15.3	14.6	16.4
Service total	6.1	9.1	2.3	6.3	10.9	13.4	14.3	17.8

NOTE: Personnel in DoD occupation code 9 are excluded (i.e., trainees and personnel who are hospitalized or in military prison).

The table also shows the extent of differential change among occupations between the prewar and postwar periods. Army occupations rose 2–4 percentage points, while Air Force changes were a bit more diverse. For example, Air Force electronic equipment repairers' rates rose from 2.1 to 5.9 percent, while electrical/mechanical equipment repairers' rates rose from 2.0 to 7.3 percent. Navy changes ranged from 2 to 3 percentage points for most occupations, and Marine Corps occupations rose 2–5 percent. The similarity of changes across occupations within a service shows that long or hostile duty stresses the entire organization—all occupations have a role to play.

There are differences in rates across occupations. Excluding medical and dental specialists, we see a range of rates in the postwar period of 7.8–11.0 percent in the Army, 5.4–9.1 percent in the Air Force, 9.2–16.3 percent in the Navy, and 10.1–25.2 percent in the Marine Corps. These ranges mark the extremes, however, and in between there are clusters of occupations with little difference, especially in the Army and Air Force. Thus, for many occupations within a service, the differences lie within two or three percentage points. Still, because these small differences persist, as seen by the similarity in occupational rankings before and after the Gulf War, they generate more extensive differences by occupation when viewed over a longer period. This will be shown below by incidence over 24 months.

Though not shown, quarter-to-quarter rates moved similarly for Navy and Marine Corps occupations; the rates rose or fell by the same amount for each occupation. By comparison, the Army and Air Force had more quarter-to-quarter variation in occupational rates. Whereas the crew of a Navy ship remains the same throughout a deployment, the character of Army and Air Force deployed units can change as a scenario unfolds. For instance, engineers may be among the first deployed, establishing the base infrastructure. Next might come the supply and quartermaster personnel, followed by the MPs. This phased utilization of specialized personnel may be responsible for differences in monthly rates across occupations.

Long or hostile duty rates are lowest among medical and dental specialists. The cause of this probably lies in the role these health-care specialists play in providing on-base care to military personnel and their families, i.e., the requirements for health care specialists include a significant component for on-base health care in addition to operational contingencies. As a result, the percentage of health care specialists separated or deployed to a hostile area in a given month is lower than for other occupational categories. In addition, policy requires the evacuation of wounded from battle areas, so many health-care personnel are stationed base hospitals rather than in the battle theater.

Total Versus Unit Rates

We expect long or hostile total rates to exceed unit rates, and Figure 3.5 confirms this. The solid line graphs the total rate, the dotted line graphs the unit rate.

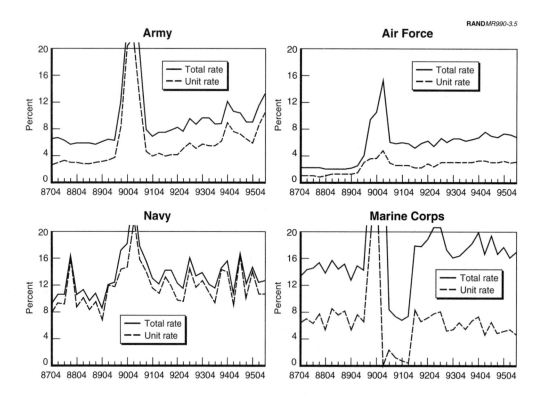

Figure 3.5—Total Versus Unit Long or Hostile Duty Rates by Service

The chart shows that the Army total rate exceeds the unit rate by a factor of two for much of the period, though after 1993 the difference narrowed. By the second quarter of 1995 more of the Army's long or hostile duty was unit-based, consistent with units being deployed to Bosnia. For the Air Force, the ratio of total to unit perstempo has remained fairly constant at about two, over a period when both measures basically doubled. The Navy has by far the closest relationship between total and unit rates, which reflects the nature of manning ships—the level and composition of crews is largely determined by the class of vessel and its range of missions. For the Marine Corps, a large gap appears between total and unit rates, but this aberration occurs because the Marine Corps unit rate reflects an undercount (Chapter 2). The Marine Corps total and unit rates are probably much closer, though not as close as for the Navy.

Incidence over 24 Months

Sooner or later, many personnel have long or hostile duty. In fact, one-third to two-thirds of personnel have such duty over 24 months, in comparison with monthly rates of around 6–16 percent.

Figures 3.6 and 3.7 show the incidence of long or hostile duty over 24 months for the Army and Air Force, respectively. Each figure contains three bars indicating the percentage having hostile perstempo (upper bar), the percentage having long, nonhostile perstempo (middle bar, labeled "long"), and either (bottom bar). The top and middle bars do not sum to the bottom bar because personnel can have both hostile and long, nonhostile duty.

The 24-month incidence of long or hostile duty differs by service and first-term/early-career. Generally, the incidence is about 40 percent for Army personnel, one-third for Air Force personnel, over two-thirds for Navy first-term personnel and nearly half for Navy early-career personnel, and over half for Marine Corps personnel.

The Army and Air Force have similar patterns of 24-month incidence, as do the Navy and Marine Corps. The Air Force has a somewhat higher hostile incidence and lower overall incidence than the Army, yet for both services about one-fifth to one-sixth of personnel experience hostile duty. The Army has a higher incidence of long, non-hostile duty, an outcome probably influenced by the stationing of Army troops in Korea. Finally, relatively little overlap occurs between hostile and long, nonhostile duty, as the overall incidence is only a bit lower than the sum of the incidences of hostile and long, nonhostile duty. This may be seen by visually adding the hostile and long, nonhostile bars in Figure 3.2 and comparing the sum to the lower bar.

The opposite is true for the Navy and, to a lesser extent, the Marine Corps (Figure 3.7). (This figure uses a different scale than Figure 3.6.) Among Navy first-term personnel, the incidence is 69 percent overall, 41 percent hostile, and 65 percent nonhostile. Thus, the sum of hostile and nonhostile (41 percent + 65 percent) is far

RAND*MR990-3.6*

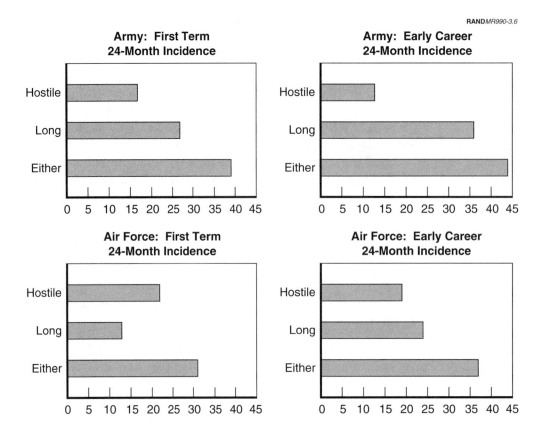

Figure 3.6—Incidence of Army and Air Force Long or Hostile Duty in 24 Months
Circa 1993–1995

greater than the overall incidence (69 percent), which indicates that many persons have both hostile and nonhostile duty. The figures for the Marine Corps first term are 61 percent overall, 23 percent hostile, and 54 percent nonhostile,[3] respectively. These patterns also hold for Navy and Marine Corps early career personnel, though with a lower hostile incidence rate. Navy and Marine Corps patterns probably reflect vessels sailing into and out of hostile waters during their deployments, so that being deployed brings exposure to both hostile and nonhostile duty.

24-Month Incidence by Occupation

Tables 3.2–3.4 show the hostile, long nonhostile, and overall incidence by occupation. We find considerable variation across occupations in the Army, Air Force, and Marine Corps for hostile and long nonhostile incidence. The Navy, in contrast, shows more consistency, though there are differences here, too. For example, the overall first-term incidence ranges from 25 to 46 percent across Army occupations, 8

---

[3]Marine Corps nonhostile duty is undercounted (Chapter 2).

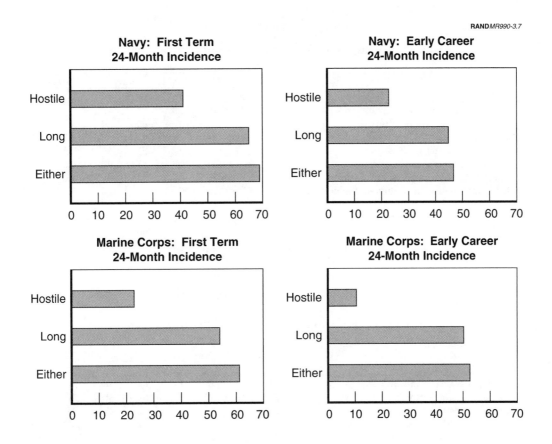

Figure 3.7—Incidence of Navy and Marine Corps Long or Hostile Duty in 24-Months
Circa 1993–1995

Table 3.2

Incidence of Hostile Duty in 24 Months by Occupation

	Army		Air Force		Navy		Marines	
Occupation	1st	EC	1st	EC	1st	EC	1st	EC
Infantry, gun crews, and seamanship	20	14	37	32	49	25	32	22
Electronic equipment repairers	15	12	19	19	36	26	17	7
Communications and intelligence	16	14	17	16	45	24	27	17
Medical and dental specialists	12	8	4	6	13	9	NA	NA
Other technical and allied specialists	11	11	23	16	30	15	6	9
Functional support and administration	11	9	15	15	37	20	13	5
Electrical/mechanical equipment repairers	17	15	30	26	48	25	21	11
Craftsmen	32	29	21	20	39	22	15	5
Service and supply handlers	21	16	29	19	47	26	17	7
Total	17	13	22	19	41	23	23	11

NOTE: 1st = personnel at their first-term reenlistment decision point, and EC = early career, i.e., personnel beyond first term and with 10 or fewer years of service, at their reenlistment decision point. NA=not applicable.

Table 3.3

Incidence of Long Nonhostile Duty in 24 Months by Occupation

Occupation	Army		Air Force		Navy		Marines	
	1st	EC	1st	EC	1st	EC	1st	EC
Infantry, gun crews, and seamanship	30	37	19	28	77	45	75	63
Electronic equipment repairers	28	40	13	27	62	54	45	47
Communications and intelligence	27	37	11	23	67	40	42	55
Medical and dental specialists	18	26	4	14	21	16	NA	NA
Other technical and allied specialists	17	34	14	26	43	32	25	44
Functional support and administration	22	31	9	18	62	37	37	39
Electrical/mechanical equipment repairers	31	41	15	29	72	50	53	54
Craftsmen	25	36	13	32	74	46	41	46
Service and supply handlers	28	38	17	26	80	49	43	47
Total	27	36	13	24	65	45	54	50

NOTE: 1st = personnel at their first-term reenlistment decision point, and EC = early career, i.e., personnel beyond first term and with 10 or fewer years of service, at their reenlistment decision point. NA=not applicable.

Table 3.4

Incidence of Long or Hostile Duty in 24 Months by Occupation

Occupation	Army		Air Force		Navy		Marines	
	1st	EC	1st	EC	1st	EC	1st	EC
Infantry, gun crews, and seamanship	44	45	49	50	81	48	81	66
Electronic equipment repairers	38	46	27	39	68	56	51	48
Communications and intelligence	38	46	24	34	72	43	54	61
Medical and dental specialists	27	32	8	19	27	19	NA	NA
Other technical and allied specialists	25	42	33	37	49	37	28	47
Functional support and administration	30	37	22	29	65	39	42	41
Electrical/mechanical equipment repairers	42	49	39	45	75	52	60	56
Craftsmen	46	51	30	45	76	48	48	48
Service and supply handlers	42	48	42	39	83	51	49	49
Total	39	44	31	37	69	47	61	53

NOTE: 1st = personnel at their first-term reenlistment decision point, and EC = early career, i.e., personnel beyond first term and with 10 or fewer years of service, at their reenlistment decision point. NA=not applicable.

to 49 percent across Air Force occupations, 27 to 83 percent across Navy occupations, and 28 to 81 percent across Marine Corps occupations. Hostile incidence for Army first-term personnel is 11 percent in functional support and administration, 20 percent in combat arms, and 32 percent in craftsmen. For first term Marine Corps combat arms, the incidence of long nonhostile duty is 75 percent, while that of hostile duty is 32 percent. Early-career communications and intelligence specialists have a hostile incidence of 14 percent in the Army, 16 percent in the Air Force, 24 percent in the Navy, and 17 percent in the Marine Corps.

Months of Long or Hostile Duty in 24 Months

Table 3.5 displays median months of long or hostile perstempo over 24 months among personnel with a positive incidence. Median months are typically 6–7 in the Navy, fewer among first-term Marines, and often 3–4 months in all other cases, i.e.,

Table 3.5

Median Months of Long or Hostile Duty in 24 Months

Occupation	Army 1st	Army EC	Air Force 1st	Air Force EC	Navy 1st	Navy EC	Marines 1st	Marines EC
Infantry, gun crews, and seamanship	4	4	5	4	7	6	7	6
Electronic equipment repairers	4	3	3	3	6	6	6	4
Communications and intelligence	4	3	3.5	3	7	7	5	4
Medical and dental specialists	4	4	3.5	2	5	6	NA	NA
Other technical and allied specialists	3	3	4	2	6	6	2	3
Functional support and administration	4	3	4	3	7	7	6	3
Electrical/mechanical equipment repairers	4	4	4	3	8	6	6	5
Craftsmen	3	3	3	3	8	7	3	3
Service and supply handlers	4	4	4	3	7	7	6	3

NOTE: 1st = personnel at their first-term reenlistment decision point, and EC = early career, i.e., personnel beyond first term and with 10 or fewer years of service, at their reenlistment decision point. NA=not applicable.

early-career Marines, and first-term and early-career Army and Air Force personnel. Thus, Navy and many first-term Marine Corps personnel with a positive incidence can anticipate being away over a fourth of the time over 24 months, while others can anticipate being away 12–16 percent of the time.

We also tabulated median months of hostile duty among personnel who had some. These were generally a month less than the corresponding figures in Table 3.5 and are not shown.

Total and Hostile Episodes in 24 Months

Tables 3.6 and 3.7 show episodes for first-term and early-career personnel, respectively. Each table has two columns for each service; the first column gives the percentages having none, one, two, or three or more total episodes, and the second column shows the distribution of hostile versus nonhostile episodes given the total number of episodes.

Among Army first-term personnel, 61 percent have no episodes and 29 percent have one, leaving about 10 percent with two or more episodes. Also, as the number of episodes increases, the percentage of hostile episodes increases. The Air Force first-term pattern is similar to the Army's: 69 percent have no episodes, 23 percent have one episode, 7 percent have two or more episodes, and the percentage of hostile episodes increases with total episodes. However, Air Force personnel with two or more episodes have a high proportion of multiple hostile episodes. Of personnel with two episodes, for 56 percent both episodes are hostile, and of (the small number of) personnel with three or more episodes, 63 percent have three or more hostile episodes.

The Navy and Marine Corps again have similar rates. Only 31 percent of Navy and 39 percent of Marine Corps first-term personnel have no episodes. Compared with the

Table 3.6

Episodes of Long or Hostile Duty in 24 Months Circa 1993–1995:
Total and Hostile Episodes, First Term
(percentages)

Episodes	Army Total	Army Hostile	Air Force Total	Air Force Hostile	Navy Total	Navy Hostile	Marine Corps Total	Marine Corps Hostile
None	61.4		69.3		31.2		39.0	
One	29.1	100	22.9	100	23.1	100	34.1	100
0 hostile		61.1		32.7		54.4		68.2
1 hostile		38.9		67.4		45.6		31.8
Two	7.9	100	5.9	100	25.6	100	20.5	100
0 hostile		41.5		15.7		37.4		55.8
1 hostile		33.8		28.3		53.2		33.0
2 hostile		24.7		56.0		9.4		11.3
Three plus	1.6	100	1.9	100	20.2	100	6.4	100
0 hostile		30.3		13.6		28.0		50.1
1 hostile		31.2		9.9		54.5		33.2
2 hostile		26.0		13.1		16.2		13.1
3+ hostile		12.5		63.4		1.3		3.6
Total	100		100		100		100	

Table 3.7

Episodes of Long or Hostile Duty in 24 Months Circa 1993–1995:
Total and Hostile Episodes, Early Career
(percentages)

Episodes	Army Total	Army Hostile	Air Force Total	Air Force Hostile	Navy Total	Navy Hostile	Marine Corps Total	Marine Corps Hostile
None	56.3		62.9		31.2		52.7	
One	30.1	100	25.5	100	23.1	100	19.8	100
0 hostile		74.6		54.2		54.4		61.2
1 hostile		25.4		45.9		45.6		38.8
Two	11.0	100	8.0	100	25.6	100	16.1	100
0 hostile		63.7		40.9		37.4		46.3
1 hostile		25.3		29.8		53.2		45.8
2 hostile		11.0		29.4		9.4		7.9
Three or more	2.6	100	3.6	100	20.2	100	11.4	100
0 hostile		47.9		19.5		28.0		39.2
1 hostile		29.7		17.7		54.5		44.7
2 hostile		14.0		17.2		16.2		14.1
3+ hostile		8.4		45.6		1.3		2.1
Total	100		100		100		100	

Army and Air Force, the percentage with two or more episodes is high: 46 percent of Navy and 27 percent of Marines have two or more episodes. Here, too, the percentage of hostile episodes increases as total episodes increase.

The same picture largely holds for early careerists (Table 3.7). The main difference is a minor one related to the Marine Corps; nearly 53 percent of early-career Marines have no episodes versus 39 percent of first-term Marines. This reflects the Marine Corps force structure, where a large portion of combat personnel are in the first term, and the high incidence of long or hostile duty among those personnel (Table 3.4).

This completes our description of long- or hostile-duty trends and levels. We have examined monthly rates, compared total and unit rates, and presented monthly rates by occupation. We have also described the 24-month incidence for hostile duty, long nonhostile duty, and the union of the two, by service, occupation, and first-term/early-career status. Finally, we have presented information about months and episodes over 24 months. With this background, we proceed to analyze the effect of long or hostile duty on reenlistment.

Chapter Four

A MODEL OF DEPLOYMENT AND REENLISTMENT

OVERVIEW

Our model places perstempo in a dynamic retention model developed in earlier RAND work.[1] The model, presented in Appendix A, focuses on the relationship between deployment, promotion, and retention, where deployment includes military operations, overseas tours, vessel deployments, and training and exercises. The model assumes that a service member's satisfaction derived from military service is a function of expected and actual deployment, and therefore deployment affects the reenlistment decision. Expected and actual deployment directly affect the expected utility of remaining in service, and indirectly affect it through the possible effect on promotion speed. The model accounts for a person's:

- taste for military service

- preference for deployment

- value of continuing in service versus leaving

- efforts to maximize that value.

At the outset of a term of service, a person forms expectations about the frequency, duration, and risks of deployment and the satisfaction that deployment may bring. These expectations influence the choice of service and choice of occupation. The model accounts for service/occupation bundling together many different attributes, each of which could affect the individual's level of satisfaction. The individual seeks to choose the best bundle given his or her preferences and the choices available. Because of the bundling, some attributes may be present in higher or lower quantities than the individual would prefer if they could be freely chosen. In particular, the *expected* level of deployment may be greater or less than the *preferred* level.

Subsequently, during the term, there is a realization of deployment. This *actual* level may not be equal to the expected or preferred levels. The actual level may result in increased satisfaction for some but reduced satisfaction for others. Thus, the model

---

[1] Beth J. Asch and John T. Warner, *A Theory of Military Compensation and Personnel Policy*, MR-439-OSD, RAND Corporation, Santa Monica, Calif., 1994.

accounts for actual deployment possibly being too much of a good thing. Even for the person who regards expected deployment with positive anticipation because it will be near the preferred level, too much actual deployment can reduce the level of satisfaction.

At the end of the period, the individual takes stock and makes a decision to stay or leave. The decision depends on expected and actual deployment. Expected deployment had guided the choice of service and occupation, and actual deployment is used to update the expectations. The actual level of deployment may cause the individual to adjust his or her expectations about the extent, nature, and predictability of future deployment. In addition, since new enlistees have no first-hand knowledge of deployment, the deployment experience enables the enlistee to learn whether he or she likes it, i.e., whether it is a satisfying and fulfilling experience.

Figure 4.1 depicts the relationship between deployment and satisfaction (or utility). Though it graphs one of many possible relationships, the figure shows a case in which satisfaction first rises and then declines as the amount of deployment increases. This accords with an underlying assumption (for this figure) that the person is risk-averse and that deployment enters the utility function quadratically. Further, the figure distinguishes between expected and preferred levels of deployment. Here, the expected level is less than the preferred level:

- The actual level of deployment, not shown, might be zero, in which case the person is less well off than expected;

- It could be in the preferred range, leaving the person better off than expected; or

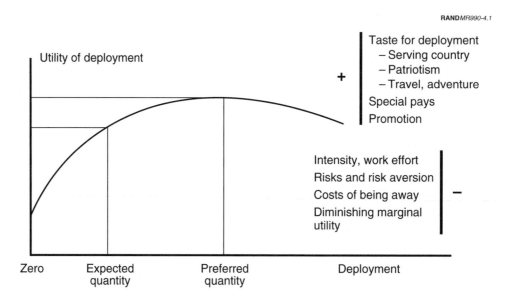

Figure 4.1—Deployment and Utility

- It could lie well beyond the preferred level, resulting in lower satisfaction than expected and, for extensive deployment, in a level of satisfaction below that for zero deployment.

Finally, the figure notes other factors that affect the satisfaction derived from deployment, e.g., the effect on promotion, special pays, predictability, risks, work effort, and personal costs of deployment.

The stay/leave decision also depends on one's preference for military service, expected future military earnings, expected civilian earnings, and random unanticipated factors other than those associated with deployment.

In addition, the model accounts for other aspects often cited in discussions of deployment:

- The individual can exert effort to change expected deployment, e.g., by volunteering for a mission or transferring to a unit more or less likely to deploy, and the model includes the cost and benefit of such effort.

- The model allows deployment to affect promotion speed, which affects the expected value of remaining in the military. If deployment provides leadership opportunities and increases skills and knowledge, it can increase the speed of promotion. But deployment might delay someone from attending training or obtaining education required for promotion, thereby delaying promotion.

- Deployments vary. Some involve hectic activity and hard work, while others are not stressful. The model can incorporate these variations to handle different kinds of deployments, e.g., peace enforcement, peacekeeping, humanitarian aid, or generic dimensions of deployments, e.g., weather, risk of chemical or biological weapons, terrain, mission (water purification, combat, air cover), and so forth.

- Deployment may create additional work for personnel who remain home. Deploying units may be brought up to strength at the expense of other units on post; however, the workload of the unit remaining behind may not decrease. Indeed, if the deploying unit is of a like kind, for example, military police, the workload might increase when the stay-behind unit has fewer people to accomplish it. The model can account for this; the more individual effort required, the higher the individual cost, and the more likely a negative impact on retention.

- Finally, the model can account for the effect of variable pays such as Family Separation Allowance, Hostile Fire Pay, and reenlistment bonuses. The services frequently employ such pays to compensate for hazardous or arduous conditions and to improve retention of critical skills.

GUIDANCE FROM THEORY

The theory suggests several observations useful to understanding the empirical work reported in the next chapter:

- *Individuals enter military service with expectations about the training, locations, assignments, perstempo, and risks they will encounter.* We control for these expectations by estimating reenlistment models separately by service and including occupation as an explanatory variable. Further, these expectations may affect the decision to enlist, choice of service, and choice of military occupation. As a result, they affect the selection of individuals into a service and occupation. This means that the "effect" of occupation on reenlistment not only includes the effect of expectations associated with being in an occupation, but also the response of the typical person in the occupation. One occupation might have high expected perstempo and attract personnel who desire high perstempo, while another occupation has low perstempo and attracts personnel who prefer low perstempo. The occupation effect, then, represents expectations and sorting. In addition, the selection effect can affect the other coefficients, including the response to long or hostile duty. Personnel in special forces may respond very positively to hazardous or extensive assignments, for example.

- *The perstempo variables represent perstempo outcomes relative to expectations.* With occupation indicators controlling for the expected duties within an occupation, the long or hostile duty variables represent outcomes holding expectations constant. Further, expectations account for the possibility of no long or hostile duty; the expected number of episodes may be 0.5, say. But individual personnel have different outcomes—months and episodes of perstempo—despite their being in the same occupation and service, and therefore presumably having similar expectations. We use these diverse outcomes in estimating the effect of long or hostile duty on reenlistment.

  Surveys of youth attitudes about the military provide insight into why long or hostile duty might have a positive effect on reenlistment. Compared to youth in general, youth who enlist are more likely to cite travel and duty to country as reasons for joining the military (Appendix B). If so, duty involving separation from home or hostile duty may fulfill these expectations. By the same token, an outcome without long or hostile duty may represent a lack of fulfillment.

  Our results agree with that view. Empirically, the *incidence* of long or hostile duty is associated with higher reenlistment, compared to having none. In effect, personnel who had such duty typically had positive outcomes relative to their expectations, while others had negative outcomes relative to their expectations. Thus the contrast between persons with and without long or hostile duty is a contrast between persons who ex ante may have had the same expectations but who, by the end of their term, have divided into winners and losers.

- *Personnel having no long or hostile duty not only have unfulfilled expectations but also may have a heavier workload than they expected.* This would reinforce the winners/losers distinction. When personnel leave for long separations or duty in hostile areas, the workload at their home base does not necessarily decrease. If units regularly rotate out to deploy while others return from deployment to take their place, then the existing workload can be handled smoothly. The Navy, and to a large degree the Marine Corps, typifies this behavior. But if separation/deployment is hard to predict, as in the Army and Air Force, then units remaining on base may have to cope with higher variation in their workload and periods of unusually high workload. This burden can be exacerbated if remaining units are short-handed because some of their personnel have been attached to deploying units. These workload effects (more variance, higher levels) may lead to higher stress and longer hours, making the experience of remaining home even less attractive than expected. By implication, the effect of separation/deployment on reenlistment may be more positive in comparison to having no separation or deployment.

- *Long or hostile duty can have a direct effect on reenlistment and an indirect effect operating though promotion.* The *immediate* satisfaction or dissatisfaction from long or hostile duty is not directly relevant to reenlistment; from the standpoint of reenlistment, it represents the past. But that duty has relevance to the reenlistment decision in two ways: to update expectations, giving better information about what to expect in the future *and* whether it will be to the service member's liking; and to speed or slow promotion. Long or hostile duty can provide unique circumstances for demonstrating one's proficiency, leadership potential, and ability to work in a team. It may also lead to awards and decorations. These elements—performance and awards—contribute favorably to promotion evaluations. The long or hostile duty coefficients in the regression model incorporate both effects, i.e., updating expectations and affecting promotion speed.

- *Long or hostile duty generates individual costs of adjustment.* These will be factored into expectations updating and include, for example, the loss of close contact with family and friends, concern about burdens placed on one's nondeploying spouse (e.g., household responsibilities, child care), making arrangements to have belongings monitored and bills paid (late payment of bills can affect credit rating), and possibly missing military education and training required for career development and promotion. The greater the extent of long or hostile duty, the greater the disruption. Although we find (Chapter 5) the incidence of such duty has a positive effect on reenlistment, we also find that more months erodes this effect.

- *Personnel are not indifferent to hostile duty.* Because it carries greater risk of injury or death, hostile duty should have a more negative effect on reenlistment than nonhostile duty. This simple but important observation recognizes that the nature of perstempo can make a difference in reenlistment. In many cases, hostile duty does have a more negative effect on reenlistment than nonhostile duty.

- *Early-career personnel should be considered a selected group relative to first-term personnel.* Personnel who choose to continue beyond the first term presumably have a close fit between their preferred and offered military opportunities. Also, their first-term experiences will likely have been positive, including long or hostile duty. Compared with first-term personnel, early careerists are better informed about the rigors of military service and probably have more-accurate expectations about service life, including deployments and overseas basing. Their positive experience and self-selection suggest that early careerists know more about what to expect and will be less influenced by new assignments than first-term personnel. The findings support this: long or hostile duty has less effect on reenlistment for early careerists than first-term personnel. In particular, the incidence of long or hostile duty still has a positive effect upon first-termers, but the extent (number of months or episodes) barely reduces that effect.

- *The suggestion that long or hostile duty will exert stronger effects where the incidence and extent are higher—namely, the Navy and Marine Corps—is mistaken.* It confuses the formation of expectations with the impact of outcomes (actual experience). Expectations are formed in every service and occupation; accordingly, outcomes can differ from expectations in every service and occupation. In fact, Navy long or hostile duty, though high by our 24-month measures, is quite predictable because it derives from the deployment of ships under the Navy's deployment/home-port rotation policy.[2] In contrast, long or hostile duty in the Army and Air Force has changed since the late 1980s and may be more difficult to predict than in the Navy. Despite the differences in level, the effect of long or hostile duty on reenlistment has many similarities across the services. Even so, effects appear weaker in the Navy, where personnel presumably can form more-accurate expectations beforehand and are less subject to large variance from those expectations.

- *Because we are interested in the effect of long or hostile duty on reenlistment, we want duty variation to be exogenous to the individual.* Variations usually result from experiences outside the service member's control, but individuals can influence their assignments by volunteering for duty or transferring to units more or less likely to separate or deploy. These actions probably occur on a small scale and should have little effect on our results. If persons who were more likely to cause a change in their long or hostile duty were more likely to reenlist, the estimated effect of such duty on reenlistment would be biased. But conditions and outcomes are not that clear-cut. According to theory, differences between individuals in their valuation of long or hostile duty, positive or negative, will induce some persons to reduce the amount of such duty and others to increase it. These actions are not necessarily associated—positively or negatively—with a propensity to reenlist. As a result, the effect of self-determined duty on the estimated coefficients is indeterminate. Given this indeterminacy and the likely small scale of self-determined long or hostile duty, we believe our results show the effect of that duty on reenlistment with reasonable accuracy.

- *The estimated effect of long or hostile duty on reenlistment also includes the effect of related compensation.* We have derived measures from data on the receipt of Family Separation Allowance and Hostile Fire Pay, special pays contingent on long separation and hostile duty. Therefore, when our data indicate such duty,

---

[2]Surveys could be used to learn about expectations at the time of enlistment and at subsequent points, e.g., at reenlistment or after a unit deployment or hostile episode. This would allow comparison of expectations in the Navy versus other services, for instance. We thank David Chu for this suggestion.

they often indicate the receipt of FSA, HFP, or both.[3] Thus, the estimated effects must be considered as including FSA and HFP. Since FSA is paid to partially reimburse personnel with dependents for expenses resulting from a 30-day or longer separation and HFP is paid for duty involving imminent danger, FSA and HFP are meant to compensate for cost and risk. We therefore expect them to offset or reduce negative aspects associated with long or hostile duty, and consequently to make the estimated effect of perstempo on reenlistment more positive. Finally, because FSA and HFP are fixed in amount (FSA II is $75 per month and HFP is $150 per month), it is not possible to estimate the separate effect of higher or lower levels of FSA and HFP on reenlistment, though it would be desirable to do so.

Other compensation-related factors also exist. "For example, reenlisting in a contingency area allows one to receive Selective Reenlistment Bonuses tax free, and some services offer a station-of-choice reassignment option to those members who reenlist while in deployed status. Both serve to encourage a favorable reenlistment decision while serving in a contingency area."[4]

The empirical analysis of long or hostile duty on reenlistment, the subject of the next chapter, will be based on this theory and its implications.

---

[3]An exception to this occurs when the DMDC unit separated/deployed indicator is used to impute long, nonhostile duty to personnel without dependents. These personnel receive no special pay for long, non-hostile duty.

[4]Communication to the author from the Office of Officer and Enlisted Personnel Management, Office of the Secretary of Defense, September 9, 1998.

Chapter Five

REGRESSION ANALYSIS OF LONG OR HOSTILE DUTY AND REENLISTMENT

Constructing measures that are relevant to the individual is important for studying the effect of long or hostile duty on reenlistment. The best way to do this is to follow a number of approaches, the common element being cumulative duty over a 24-month period. Our main variables are the incidence, months, and episodes of long or hostile duty in 24 months; we also consider duty related to unit deployment. We do not use the monthly perstempo rate because it has little relevance to the individual; in a given month, most personnel have no long or hostile duty, and month-to-month variations in the monthly rate have little relationship to an individual's cumulating experience.

We find a common story in the different approaches. Having some long or hostile duty rather than none increases reenlistment. This positive effect, however, is reduced as total and hostile months of duty increase. The reduction occurs prominently among first-term personnel and weakly (if at all) among early-career personnel. With respect to episodes, personnel with at least one nonhostile episode are much more likely to reenlist than those with no episode. But as more of the episodes are hostile, the positive effect of episodes on reenlistment declines and may turn negative.

ESTIMATION METHOD

We use a logit specification relating the probability of reenlistment to a set of explanatory variables. The logit model has the form:

$$p = \frac{1}{1 + e^{-\beta' x_i}}$$

where p = probability of reenlistment and x_i = explanatory variables. Although the reenlistment probability is not directly observed, the logit probability expression is used to form a sample likelihood in terms of the explanatory variables and their effects, β. Maximizing the likelihood produces estimates of β and its standard errors.

In addition to months and episodes, the explanatory variables include the Armed Forces Qualification Test (AFQT) score category, education level, race/ethnicity, and one-digit primary occupation. AFQT and education are the customary indicators of recruit quality, and race/ethnicity, like AFQT and education, help control for military/civilian differences in compensation and career opportunity. The occupation indicators control for differences in the expected level of long or hostile duty by occupation, as suggested by the differences across occupations (Tables 3.1–3.4).[1]

Below, we discuss results from the regression analyses and predict the percentage of personnel whose reenlistment has been negatively affected by their actual amount of long or hostile duty. We also predict the effect of higher levels of duty for the Army, Air Force, and Marine Corps, and the effect of capped months for the Navy. Finally, we sketch the results of additional data analyses done to confirm or qualify the robustness of our findings. (Appendix C contains a description of the analysis file, variable means and standard errors, and full regression results.)

RESULTS

Months

Table 5.1 displays the regression coefficients for incidence, total months, and hostile months by service for first-term and early-career personnel. In the regressions, incidence is indicated by a dummy variable that takes the value "1" if the person had any long or hostile duty during the 24-month period culminating six months prior to the end of term, and takes the value "0" otherwise. Because hostile months enter the regression as a separate variable, the coefficient on total months is the effect of nonhostile months on reenlistment. The coefficient on hostile months shows the difference between the effect of nonhostile months and hostile months, and the full effect of hostile months is the sum of the total months and hostile months coefficients. We chose this parameterization to test directly whether the effect of hostile months differs from that of nonhostile months. Finally, a positive regression coefficient implies a positive effect on the reenlistment probability, and a negative coefficient implies a negative effect.

The incidence coefficients are positive and generally large enough to indicate a major difference in the reenlistment probability of personnel having or not having long or hostile duty. The incidence coefficients are small only for first-term reenlistment in the Air Force and Marine Corps. We know, however, that the Marine Corps first-term results should be viewed cautiously because of the undercount (Chapter 2). The small Air Force effect suggests that long or hostile duty is not seen as positively as in

---

[1]Because we are dealing with reenlistment at a given point in time, we cannot estimate some effects even though it would be desirable to do so. For instance, at any point in time there is no variation in the military basic pay table, average civilian pay, unemployment rate, and reenlistment bonuses. Therefore, the effects of these variables enter the constant term of the regression. Further, the explanatory variables do not control for an individual's expected promotion speed (e.g., fast or slow rate of promotions), and hence the individual's present discounted value of expected military pay, or the individual's specific civilian pay and job opportunities.

Table 5.1

Perstempo Coefficients in Reenlistment Regressions
(standard errors in parentheses)

Variable	Army 1st	Army EC	Air Force 1st	Air Force EC	Navy 1st	Navy EC	Marine Corps 1st	Marine Corps EC
Incidence dummy	.584*	.461*	.069	.458*	.203*	.318*	.068	.468*
	(.034)	(.030)	(.045)	(.033)	(.051)	(.038)	(.050)	(.064)
Total months	−.030*	−.035*	−.025*	−.006	−.019*	−.005	.005	−.019*
	(.004)	(.004)	(.007)	(.005)	(.005)	(.005)	(.006)	(.009)
Hostile months	−.086*	−.030*	.008	−.016*	−.054*	−.010	−.033*	−.030
	(.008)	(.007)	(.009)	(.007)	(.011)	(.011)	(.014)	(.024)

NOTE: 1st = personnel at their first term reenlistment decision point, and EC = early career = personnel beyond first term and with 10 or fewer years of service, at their reenlistment decision point. Level of significance: * = .05 or better.

the Army and Navy. Perhaps this is because our data do not control for short, nonhostile duty, and such duty may be quite similar to long, nonhostile duty in the Air Force—hence less contrast between some long or hostile duty and no such duty.

In contrast to incidence, total months generally have a negative effect on reenlistment, and hostile months tend to have an even greater negative effect.

The coefficients present a consistent picture across the services and first-term/early-career groups. For instance, at the Army first-term reenlistment point, each month reduces the dependent variable (the log odds of reenlisting) by −.030, and for each hostile month another −.086 is taken away. The same pattern is true for Army early-career personnel, Air Force first-term and early-career personnel (except hostile months, first-term), Navy first-term and early-career personnel, and Marine Corps first-term and early-career personnel (except total months, first-term).

As discussed, the data undercount long, nonhostile months and episodes, more for first-term personnel than early-career personnel, and most for first-term Marine Corps personnel (Chapter 2). The undercount can affect both the incidence and months coefficients, but it is likely the incidence undercount is small (because there are 24 months over which to detect *any* incidence) with the possible exception of first-term Marines. For months coefficients, however, the undercount probably causes a downward bias.[2] If so, the months coefficient in these cases may be biased downward; for instance, the estimated first-term Army coefficient of −.030 might in truth be −.020, a larger value.

---

[2]The undercount creates two problems: measured months are systematically less than true months, and after allowing for the systematic undercount, months contain a measurement error. If there were no measurement error, the undercount would be equivalent to a change of scale, e.g., measured months = b x true months, $0<b<1$, and the estimated coefficient would equal the true coefficient divided by b. Suppose the true coefficient were −.02 and b = .67, then the estimated coefficient would be −.02/.67 = −.03. Given this systematic bias, the measurement error probably biases the estimated coefficient toward zero, i.e., moves it back toward −.02 and possibly farther toward zero. (See Greene (1993), p. 281, eqn. 9-26). As a result of these competing effects, the net effect of the undercount is indeterminate.

Although we do not know the extent of bias, the Navy provides a point of comparison because its data have little undercount. The Navy first-term months coefficient is –.019, which compares with the Army coefficient of –.030 and Air Force's –.025, and these are statistically about the same as the Navy.[3] The Navy early-career coefficient on months, –.005, also is much larger than the Army's –.035 but insignificantly larger than the Air Force's –.006. The near-zero coefficients on months for Air Force and Navy early careerists suggest that these personnel are accustomed to, or indifferent to, separations of 30 days or longer.

The incidence and months effects for first-term Marine Corps personnel are statistically insignificant. This may be the result of the undercount, and it suggests that the first-term Marine Corps results should be viewed cautiously and perhaps disregarded. With incidence missing from many Marines who in fact had long or hostile duty and who presumably would have had a negative effect of months on reenlistment, the estimated incidence coefficient is smaller than it otherwise would have been. With a lower starting point, the effect of months becomes more horizontal, or in this case, slightly positive. In contrast, early-career Marine Corps results look similar to those for the Army.

Months and episodes must be interpreted with some care for Navy personnel. All seagoing personnel can expect to spend a significant proportion of their time underway, deployed. But because of rotation timing within our 24-month window of observation, months and episodes will differ among personnel. If all vessels strictly followed a policy of 6 months afloat and 12 months ashore, a seaman who began a deployment at the beginning of the 24-month window, returned to home port, and deployed again would have 12 months deployment in 24 months, whereas a seaman who had just arrived back in port at the beginning of the 24-month window would be there for 12 months, deploy for 6, and return home again, for a total of 6 months in 24. Over a longer window, say 3 years, months deployed would be *equal* for these two seamen (12 months in 36 months). As a result, even though differences exist in a 24-month window, we would expect the effect of months to be blurred. Nevertheless, the regression results indicate that among Navy first-term personnel who have had some long or hostile duty, the total months separated/deployed over a 24-month period prior to reenlistment does affect the reenlistment decision. Among early-career personnel, who not only have self-selected to remain in service but also are more experienced and perhaps take a longer view of anticipated sea duty than first-term personnel, total months has little effect on reenlistment.

The Navy results are consistent with Cooke, Marcus, and Quester (1992). They analyzed Navy reenlistment data covering FY1979–1988 and found several variables that had a negative effect on first-term reenlistment: percentage under way, not

---

[3]More precisely, the Navy result is not statistically different from the Air Force result but is statistically different from the Army result. Howeveer, if the Army result is biased down, then allowing for the bias would bring the result closer to the Navy's, thus making it more likely that the Army result would not be statistically different from the Navy result. Similarly, allowing for bias in the Air Force result would likely keep it within statistical equivalence to the Navy.

deployed; deployed at decision; and very long deployment.[4] All these, in terms of our measures, would add to total months, and we found months and hostile months to be negatively related to first-term reenlistment. In addition, the deployed-at-decision variable was significant, which is consistent with our finding that actual deployment over the period leading up to reenlistment makes a difference, even though expected deployment over a longer three-year window might be the same for all personnel in a seagoing rating (Navy occupation). Further, Cooke et al. found no significant variables for the reenlistment of ,nonnuclear personnel at year-of-service 8–10. Similarly, we found months and hostile months to be insignificant for Navy early-career reenlistment.[5]

Episodes

Table 5.2 shows the predicted effect of episodes on reenlistment. In this case, we have shifted to a regression specification defining perstempo in terms of episodes. The episodes specification takes the view that since each episode of long separation or hostile duty requires the service member to make arrangements for being away, the total number of episodes may itself be important. The arrangements may be with family and friends and cover the assurance of family support, pet care, payment of bills, etc. In addition, duty in hostile areas poses danger, so, as with months, we distinguish the effects of hostile episodes from nonhostile ones. Variables are created for none, one, two, or three-plus episodes, and similarly for hostile episodes.

The table presents the predicted probability of reenlistment for the different possible combinations of episodes, holding other variables at their means. As before, the other variables include AFQT category, gender, race/ethnicity, and one-digit primary military occupation. Also, we have computed (but do not present) the 95-percent confidence bands for the predictions. The bands are about ± .02 for none or one episode and widen to ± .05 for three total episodes or two or more hostile episodes.

Looking at nonhostile episodes, we find a higher probability of reenlistment if there are one or more episodes versus none. For instance, early careerists in the Navy have a reenlistment probability of .70 at no episodes and .76 at one episode. Moreover, the reenlistment probability tends to increase, or at least not decrease, as the number of nonhostile episodes increases.

---

[4]In their data, the percentage of time under way, not deployed averaged 20 percent, i.e., one in five days "in port" was spent under way, typically for predeployment training. About 30 percent of personnel made their reenlistment decision while deployed, and about 5 percent had "very long" deployments of eight months or more (Cooke et al., p. 25). The study also found that extended maintenance activity of eight months or longer reduced reenlistment among unmarried first-term personnel. Other variables, namely, time since deployment, time between deployments, short deployment, and long deployment, also had negative effects on first-term reenlistment but were not statistically significant (p. 29).

[5]Cooke et al. also comment on sea pay: "Because sea pay is contingent only upon being attached to a ship and is independent of the ship's perstempo, . . . the linkages among sea pay, perstempo, and retention are complex." Unlike sea pay, Family Separation Allowance and Hostile Fire Pay are paid upon long separation and hostile duty, respectively. Still, sea pay should be considered as part of the regular compensation received by seagoing personnel for "the ardors of sea duty" (p. 48).

Table 5.2

Predicted Probability of Reenlistment by Episodes

Total Episodes	Hostile Episodes	Army		Air Force		Navy		Marine Corps	
		1st	EC	1st	EC	1st	EC	1st	EC
None		.40	.75	.59	.71	.45	.70	.23	.70
One	None	.50	.80	.62	.80	.50	.76	.26	.75
	One	.41	.75	.56	.76	.42	.74	.23	.72
Two	None	.56	.80	.61	.82	.49	.76	.25	.80
	One	.46	.75	.56	.78	.42	.74	.22	.77
	Two	.31	.71	.57	.78	.47	.76	.18	.75
Three	None	.62	.87	.61	.87	.46	.76	.26	.84
	One	.53	.83	.56	.83	.39	.75	.22	.81
	Two	.37	.80	.57	.83	.44	.76	.19	.79
	Three	.39	.82	.59	.79	.45	.79	.19	.61

A second feature is the negative effect of hostile episodes. For any given level of total episodes, the reenlistment probability often decreases as the number of hostile episodes increases. This can be seen prominently in the Army and Marine Corps. For instance, the Army first-term reenlistment probability is .50 for one nonhostile episode and .41 for one hostile episode, and .80 and .75 respectively for early careerists. Therefore, in this respect the results of the episodes specification differ from the incidence/months specification, where the incidence is positive and the effect of hostile months is negative. Part of the difference may be due to disallowing the incidence effect to differ between hostile and nonhostile months. In future research, when more data become available, we will allow the incidence effect to differ and test whether the difference is statistically significant.

Air Force and Navy patterns differ from the Army and Marine Corps. In the Air Force, any hostile episode reduces the probability of reenlistment below that for no hostile episode, but the number of hostile episodes does not seem to matter. Perhaps this is because some air crews might fly several hostile missions in a single month and other crews fly them over several months; our data do not distinguish the real risk per episode.[6] Another possibility is that occupations/duty assignments with high expected hostile missions attract personnel seeking adventure and willing to take risk, as mentioned in our discussion of theory in Chapter Four.

In the Navy, the pattern for early careerists stands out: given a positive number of episodes, the reenlistment probability is the same regardless of whether the episodes are hostile. This suggests a basic similarity in the routine, rigors, and risks onboard vessels deployed to both hostile and nonhostile areas. As seen in Chapter Three, many Navy personnel experience both hostile and nonhostile perstempo, which is not surprising since the route to hostile waters traverses nonhostile waters. By

---

[6]A hostile episode in our data is simply a string (months separated/deployed) in which Hostile Fire Pay was received in at least one month, implying hazardous duty or duty in a hostile area at some time during the episode. Depending on episode length and the intensity of activity *during* months in the episode, one hostile episode might involve as much danger as two or three short, less-intensive hostile episodes.

comparison, Navy first-term personnel show a mixed pattern; for instance, the reenlistment probability for two nonhostile episodes is .49, dropping to .42 if one of the episodes is hostile, and rising to .47 if both episodes are hostile. This suggests that both the negative effect of danger and positive effect of self-selection are at work.

PREDICTIONS

Impact of Long or Hostile Duty on Reenlistment

Table 5.3 shows the percentages of personnel whose long or hostile duty was predicted to increase, or alternatively, reduce their reenlistment probability. The table is computed from the reenlistment regressions (Tables C.3, C.4) and the actual data for each person in our samples who had long or hostile duty. Our main findings are:

Positive or negative impact

- First-term: Over 90 percent of Army and Marine Corps personnel were positively affected by their long or hostile duty. In contrast, just under half of Navy and Air Force personnel were positively affected.

- Early career: Long or hostile duty increased the reenlistment of nearly all early-career personnel.

Size of impact

- First-term: Of the 90 percent of Army personnel who were positively affected, their reenlistment probability increased 21 percent on average. But the 10 percent negatively affected had a 13 percent decline on average. The net affect on reenlistment probability was a positive 18 percent (.90 x 21 + .10 x (-13) = 18). The net effect was 6 percent for the Marine Corps and −1 percent for the Navy and Air Force.

- Early career: All services were predicted to have a positive net effect. The effect was 6 percent for the Army, 8 percent for the Navy, and 10 percent for the Marine Corps and Air Force.

Thus, while we found evidence of long or hostile duty hurting reenlistment among some personnel, for the majority the net effect of long or hostile duty was predicted to be positive. First-term Navy and Air Force personnel are the exceptions, though in their cases the net effect of −1 percent was near zero, i.e., reenlistment was little reduced overall. Still, over half of first-term Navy and Air Force personnel were predicted to have a negative effect, so it would not be surprising if complaints or concerns about long or hostile duty were more common in those services.

Table 5.3

Predicted Effect of Long or Hostile Duty on Reenlistment
(percent)

Group	Positively Affected	Increase in Probability	Negatively Affected	Decrease in Probability	Net Change in Probability
First Term					
Army	90	21	10	−13	18
Navy	45	6	55	−6	−1
Marine Corps	92	7	8	−4	6
Air Force	44	1	56	−4	−1
Early Career					
Army	92	7	9	−4	6
Navy	99	8	1	−1	8
Marine Corps	99	10	1	−6	10
Air Force	99	10	1	−1	10

Adding One Episode or Three Months

We also examine the implications of the regressions by predicting the effect of a change in perstempo on reenlistment. For the Army, Air Force, and Marine Corps we explored two alternatives, adding an episode for each person, and adding three months for each person.[7] However, we took a different approach for the Navy, described below.

The effect of adding episodes or months depends on the individual's starting point. A move from zero episodes to one episode will increase the reenlistment probability, while an increase in the number of hostile episodes, given some episodes, will decrease the reenlistment probability. Similarly, an increase from zero months to positive months will increase the reenlistment probability, but the probability begins to decline as months increase, and more so as hostile months increase. This months-based decline is steady, whereas the episodes specification shows stairstep effects. Adding a nonhostile episode might incrementally increase the reenlistment probability, yet adding a hostile episode might incrementally decrease the probability.

Table 5.4 presents the results. The entries in the table are the cell-average reenlistment probability and therefore represent the expected value of a random draw of individuals in the cell.

Further, the distinction between personnel with zero and personnel with positive episodes allows us to consider various military activities that draw exclusively on one group or the other, or a mix of both groups. For instance, if an Army mission added one *nonhostile* episode to first-term personnel who had zero episodes, their average reenlistment probability would rise from .41 to .51. If the activity were restricted to personnel with positive episodes, their probability would rise from .45 to .50. If the

---

[7]We decided on three months as a typical episode's duration. This may be long for Air Force episodes, but for the sake of comparability with the Army and Marine Corps we kept the Air Force at three months.

activity required first-term personnel, one-third of whom had zero episodes and two-thirds had positive episodes, the initial probability .33 x .41 + .67 x .45 = .44 (rounded) would *rise* to .33 x .51 + .67 x .50 = .50. If a *hostile* episode were added to Army personnel with zero episodes, their reenlistment probability would change very little, from .41 to .42, and if that episode were added to personnel with positive episodes, their probability would decrease from .45 to .40. Under the one-third/two-thirds mix, the reenlistment probability would *decrease* from .44 to .41 (.33 x .42 + .67 x .40 = .41).

The table shows differences between the episodes and months columns. These occur because the underlying regression specifications differ. The episodes specification accounts for the number of different episodes but not their length, and the months specification accounts for the total number of months but not the number of episodes. For the most part, the tables present the same direction of effects for adding an episode versus adding three months, though the size of the effects differs. Because we are not asserting that one set of predictions is better than the other, the table should be viewed as an approximation of the range of change in the reenlistment probability.

Table 5.4

**Change in Average Reenlistment Probability Due to Adding One Episode
or Three Months Long or Hostile Duty**

Episodes Group	Number of Persons	Initial Probability	Add 1 Episode		Add 3 Months	
			Nonhostile	Hostile	Nonhostile	Hostile
Army						
First term						
Zero episodes	21,231	.41	.51	.42	.52	.46
Positive episodes	13,358	.45	.50	.40	.43	.37
Early career						
Zero episodes	27,559	.74	.80	.75	.80	.79
Positive episodes	21,350	.78	.80	.76	.76	.75
Air Force						
First term						
Zero episodes	14,621	.59	.62	.57	.59	.59
Positive episodes	6,465	.56	.56	.56	.54	.55
Early career						
Zero episodes	24,828	.71	.80	.75	.79	.78
Positive episodes	14,629	.79	.81	.79	.78	.78
Marine Corps						
First term						
Zero episodes	7,691	.26	.30	.26	.28	.26
Positive episodes	12,035	.24	.23	.20	.24	.22
Early career						
Zero episodes	4,491	.70	.75	.72	.78	.76
Positive episodes	4,984	.76	.80	.77	.75	.74

The table indicates that adding an episode or three months perstempo causes:

- Sizable change in Army reenlistment, the direction depending on whether the duty is hostile

- Little change in Air Force reenlistment

- Small-to-modest change in Marine Corps reenlistment.

For instance, adding a hostile episode to first-term Army personnel who have already had one or more episodes of any kind would reduce their reenlistment probability from .45 to .40, a 10-percent drop. The corresponding figures for the Marine Corps are .24 to .20, a 16-percent drop, whereas there is no change in the Air Force (see shading in Table 5.4).

Capping Long Duty in the Navy

The approach of adding an episode or three months perstempo seems inappropriate for the Navy. If our concern is an illustrative increase in long or hostile duty because of an increase in peace operations, the Navy need only dispatch vessels already deployed and under way to the operational theater. Months and episodes need not increase. Though this is a simplification, it reflects the reality of the Navy's active posture. We have therefore chosen a different approach, namely, to reduce the number of Navy personnel experiencing a high number of months over 24 months. Specifically, we ask how much the reenlistment probability of personnel in the top fifth of months would change if their months were reduced to, or capped at, the average number of months in the second quintile.[8] The capping is done in two ways: nonhostile months are capped among the population of sailors who have positive nonhostile months, and hostile months are capped among the population of sailors who have positive hostile months. Only the personnel in the top quintile are affected by the capping policy; Table 5.5 reports the results for those affected personnel.

When personnel in the top (i.e., fifth) quintile of *nonhostile* months have their months reduced to the average level of months in the fourth quintile, their first term reenlistment probability increases from .41 to .42, and their early-career reenlistment probability is virtually unchanged. (The predicted increase is 0.4 percent, which rounds to zero in the table.) Therefore, the policy of capping nonhostile months has virtually no effect on Navy reenlistment.

In contrast, capping *hostile* months has a noticeable affect on first-term reenlistment. The reenlistment probability among personnel affected by the capping policy rises from .40 to .43, or 7.5 percent. However, the increase in early-career

---

[8]Specifically, the individual's total months are reduced to the average number of months in the 60–80th percentiles of the months distribution.

Table 5.5

Change in Average Reenlistment Probability Due to Reducing Months for Navy Personnel in the Top Quintiles of Nonhostile and Hostile Months

Top Quintile Group	Number of Persons	Reenlistment Probability	
		Initial	Reduced Months
Nonhostile Months			
First term	2231	0.41	0.42
Early career	3453	0.74	0.74
Hostile Months			
First term	1655	0.40	0.43
Early career	1996	0.73	0.74

NOTE: Months are reduced to average months in the next highest quintile of months.

reenlistment is small, only 0.5 percent, which rounds up to change from .73 to .74. The positive effect of capping hostile months for first-term personnel suggests that the Navy should consider doing so provided the cost is not prohibitive.

We do not know the cost of capping nonhostile or hostile months, but high months may occur precisely because the existing level of Navy operations is cost-effective. High months may result from more training or longer deployments at sea. More training could bring readiness up to desired levels, and longer deployments could avoid the need to speed up the repair and redeployment cycle of the replacement vessel, an action that could be more costly than the prospective added loss of personnel. Still, the predictions in the table point to a potential gain from capping the number of months for first-term personnel.

DATA EXPLORATIONS

We explored a number of additional regression specifications. As a set, the results are highly consistent with the preceding discussion.

First, we explained that occupation indicators control for the expected level of perstempo in an occupation and the sorting of personnel into occupations. However, since perstempo might also differ by branch, vessel class, expeditionary unit, or wing, we wanted to control for these "functional" aspects. The Perstempo file does not contain this level of information, but by using a file in RAND's data archive we at least were able to distinguish Army personnel. When branch indicators were included along with the other variables already present (perstempo variables—incidence, total months, hostile months—AFQT category, gender, race/ethnicity, and one-digit occupation), there were few changes in the perstempo coefficients. In essence, controlling for branch produced essentially no changes in the perstempo results.

Second, one-digit occupation indicators may be insufficient to control for occupation differences within the one-digit grouping.[9] These differences could include expected perstempo and might affect the estimated perstempo effects. To test for this possibility, we controlled for occupation effects at the three-digit level.[10] These adjustments resulted in basically no difference in the other coefficients, including the perstempo effects.

Third, recognizing that Hostile Fire Pay is $150 per month and Family Separation Allowance is $75 per month, we considered a specification allowing for differential perstempo effects depending on the number of months when only HFP was received, only FSA was received, or both were received. We created perstempo variables for each of these states. This specification created problems, however. Because FSA can be received only by personnel with dependents, we also had to control for dependents status, which changes for many personnel during their term of service. The results from this specification were often statistically insignificant and unintuitive, and therefore we did not pursue it. In effect, this specification sacrifices the notion of cumulative perstempo (months or episodes) for the notion that relatively small, short-term differences in monthly pay affect reenlistment.

Fourth, we tested whether perstempo coefficients differed by dependents status. For most personnel, "dependents" means having a spouse and sometimes children; fewer than 5 percent of personnel with dependents are single parents. We tried two approaches: creating subsamples of persons who were without dependents or with dependents for the entire term, and creating a dependents indicator based on dependents status at the end of the term, the idea being that persons married by the end of their term probably had a very close friend ("near spouse") during much of the term. These specifications provide results similar to one another. The dependents status regressions are presented in Appendix D for the specification using dependents status as of the end of the term. The appendix presents coefficients for the months and episodes specifications for first-term and early-career personnel, then presents tables of coefficient differences between persons with and without dependents at the end of the term. The latter tables (Tables D.7 and D.8) include tests of whether these differences are statistically significant. In some cases, the coefficients are significantly different; however, the main pattern conforms to the discussion above.

Fifth, we added a dependents dummy to the regressions underlying the tables in this section to see whether the coefficient estimates were affected. Dependents status was defined as of the end of the term. Including the dependents dummy caused practically no change in the other coefficients, though the intercept changed. The intercept change reflects the difference in the reenlistment rate between the base group in this regression (personnel without dependents) and the contrast group (personnel with dependents). This finding parallels the finding reported in the

---

[9]We thank Richard Buddin for this suggestion.

[10]This was done by differencing the explanatory variables from their three-digit occupation means, then estimating a linear probability model on the differenced data.

preceding paragraph. Because including the dependents dummy had little effect on other coefficients, the results are not included as an appendix.

Sixth, we experimented with a specification using a variable for the proportion of months that were hostile. The results were essentially the same as for the specification using hostile months outright, and since the latter is easily interpreted we used it.

Seventh, we used the DMDC unit deployed/separated indicator to create incidence and months of *unit deployment over 24 months*. The variables were created identically for personnel regardless of their dependents status and should have shown the effect of unit deployment/separation on reenlistment. The results, presented in Table 5.6, provide strong parallels to Table 5.1. In most instances, the incidence of unit separation/deployment has a positive effect on reenlistment, and months has a negative effect; most coefficients are significant.[11] Further, the months effects are closer to zero for early-career personnel than for first-term personnel, like the finding in Table 5.1 that early-career personnel are less sensitive to months than first-term personnel. First-term Marine Corps results are the exception; the incidence effect is negative and the months effect is zero, but again this comes from the undercount of Marine unit separation/deployment.

We also added variables indicating whether any of the individual's unit perstempo involved hostile duty and whether the individual had any other hostile duty (i.e., not with his or her unit). Adding these indicators left the unit incidence and months coefficients largely unchanged.[12] The hostile duty indicators are typically negative and significant for first-term personnel and have mixed effects for early-career personnel. These results remain consistent with Table 5.1.

Table 5.6

Unit Perstempo Coefficients in Reenlistment Regressions
(standard errors in parentheses)

Variable	Army 1st	Army EC	Air Force 1st	Air Force EC	Navy 1st	Navy EC	Marine Corps 1st	Marine Corps EC
Incidence Dummy	.230*	−.056	.276*	.322*	.219*	.210*	−.188*	.615*
	(.037)	(.037)	(.090)	(.068)	(.055)	(.040)	(.076)	(.117)
Total Months	−.026*	−.013*	−.041*	−.011	−.036*	−.005	.000	−.065*
	(.005)	(.004)	(.009)	(.007)	(.006)	(.005)	(.011)	(.018)

NOTE: 1st = personnel at their first-term reenlistment decision point, and EC = early career = personnel beyond first term and with 10 or fewer years of service, at their reenlistment decision point. Total months = total months an individual is deployed with his or her unit over 24 months. Level of significance: * = .05 or better.

---

[11]The unit perstempo regression include the same explanatory variables: AFQT category, education, race/ethnicity, and one-digit occupation. The effects of these variables are the same as the results show in Appendix C for the months specification, and are not reported.

[12]Except for Army first-term personnel: for them, the incidence coefficient becomes larger and the unit hostile indicator is negative.

Chapter Six

CONCLUSION

The findings provide a number of implications for policy.

MEASURES MATTER

Results show that the incidence of long or hostile duty over a 24-month span exceeds the monthly rate by a factor of three to five. Focusing only on monthly rates would therefore miss the broad extent to which personnel are directly involved in long or hostile duty. We also found major differences between monthly total versus unit rates. This was especially noticeable for the Army and Air Force—but not for the Navy, where the majority of separation and deployment reflects crew rotations afloat or ashore. Yet, overall, an emphasis on unit rates would significantly undercount the total extent of long or hostile duty.

Recent methods of monitoring perstempo include keeping track of unit separation and deployment, but as our findings indicate, unit perstempo is not the same as total perstempo. Air Force guidelines now call for units on temporary active duty for over 120 days per year to be considered overstressed, and the Army's goal is to keep units deployed no more than 120 days a year (Weible, 1998, p. 4). While these guidelines may prove adequate, our results suggest the value of also keeping track of perstempo at an individual level, particularly for monitoring the impact of perstempo on reenlistment. At levels of temporary duty (Air Force) or deployment (Army) lower than 120 days per year, negative effects on reenlistment are possible, depending on the individual's cumulative long or hostile duty over two years or longer. For instance, an airman whose unit had temporary duty of 100 days each year for two years, and who therefore was not in an overstressed unit, might nevertheless have had enough temporary duty to affect reenlistment negatively.

Finally, perstempo measures so far do nothing to record the added burden placed on the units and service members who remain at their home base. This remains a measurement challenge.

CHANGES IN MONTHLY RATES SIGNAL LARGER CHANGES IN 24-MONTH INCIDENCE

Although we do not have time-series data on monthly versus 24-month measures, it is worth considering whether the *increase* in monthly perstempo since the Gulf War has led to a roughly proportionate increase in the 24-month incidence of long or hostile duty. Relative to the pre–Gulf War period, Air Force monthly rates have doubled, Army rates have increased by over 20 percent and were headed upward in mid-1996, and Navy and Marine Corps rates—while rising relatively less—grew in proportion to hostile duty. These changes may indicate substantial increases in 24-month incidence and its hostile/nonhostile composition.

Increases in the 24-month incidence may not be in strict proportion to increases in monthly rates. A proportionate increase would be expected only if both the average length of separation or deployment and the average time not separated or deployed remained the same, in which case a higher monthly rate necessitates using a higher fraction of personnel. But personnel and units are specialized; they equip and train for certain roles. Depending on the contingencies that emerge, some units and personnel will be used more intensively. Given a constant force structure in the short run, this means that the length or number of episodes will increase more for some personnel than for others.

By implication, the change to overall higher, more-hostile perstempo can produce quite different experiences among individuals. This again suggests the value of monitoring long or hostile duty at a disaggregate level such as occupation or branch, vessel class, expeditionary force, or wing, as well as at the individual level. The same point extends to short, nonhostile duty.

IS LONG OR HOSTILE DUTY GOOD FOR REENLISTMENT?

More varied and intense use of personnel, along with increased optempo stemming from peace operations, has fueled a debate about readiness. A key issue in the debate is whether higher perstempo has impaired readiness through a decline in the quality of military life, loss of morale, and lower retention. Some assessments support the view that higher perstempo creates higher stress among personnel (e.g., Fossen et al. (1997)), but others find a positive relationship between perstempo and reenlistment. According to the Army's Deputy Chief of Staff for Personnel, testifying before Congress in March 1997, "To date, PERSTEMPO has not impacted on retention. In fact, soldier[s] . . . in our most-deployed units are reenlisting in rates higher than those that do not deploy."[1]

Our model and findings help reconcile these contrary positions. First, we find that having some perstempo—in our case, a separation of 30 days or longer or duty in a hostile area—is in fact associated with a higher reenlistment probability, as compared with not having *any* such perstempo. This aligns with survey findings that

---

[1]LTG Frederick E. Vollrath, U.S. Army Deputy Chief of Staff for Personnel, Testimony before Senate Armed Services Subcommittee on Personnel Hearing: FY98 Defense Budget, March 5, 1997.

indicate many persons are interested in military service for adventure, travel, patriotism, and an opportunity to serve actively. It is also possible perstempo has a positive effect on promotion, as compared with no perstempo; this remains a topic for future study. Second, we find that the extent and nature of long or hostile duty matter. More months away from home, especially on hostile duty, reduce the positive impact of having long or hostile duty. Thus, both the length and danger of duty have a negative effect on reenlistment. Putting the two main findings together, we see that having some long or hostile duty has a positive effect on reenlistment, but as the duty lengthens or involves danger it may cause stress and disrupt personal life, thereby lowering morale and potentially reducing reenlistment.

WHERE IS THE MARGIN?

Knowing that longer or more dangerous duty erodes the positive reenlistment effect of having some such duty, we asked whether the 1993–1995 levels of duty had been high enough to reduce reenlistment and whether added duty would hurt reenlistment. Results indicate that the higher levels of separation and deployment prevailing during those years had relatively little negative impact on reenlistment; for those whose added duty was nonhostile, the effect was positive.

We found two groups where long or hostile duty had reduced the likelihood of re-enlistment *below what it would have been in its absence:* 55 percent of first-term Air Force personnel were negatively affected, as were 56 percent of first-term Navy personnel. For all other groups fewer than 10 percent of personnel were negatively affected.

We explored the effect of adding more long or hostile duty to Army, Air Force, and Marine Corps personnel beyond the levels of 1993–1995. We found that the added duty caused effects that varied by whether the duty was hostile, and whether it was added to personnel who had already had, or not had, some such duty.

We estimate that adding a hostile episode to personnel who have already had at least one episode over a 24-month period would reduce their first-term reenlistment rate by 5 percent in the Army (from 45 to 40 percent) and by 4 percent in the Marine Corps. In other words, among these personnel the added episode would result in one service member in nine not reenlisting in the Army, and one service member in six not reenlisting in the Marine Corps. We found no such effect for Air Force personnel, though that may be because our measures miss a significant fraction of Air Force perstempo, i.e., activities and missions in nonhostile areas that do not require a separation from home base of 30 days or more.

The 5 percent and 4 percent changes for the Army and Marine Corps may be considered large compared to, say, a 5-percent increase in basic military pay relative to civilian pay. Such a large relative pay increase can be expected to increase the first-term reenlistment rate by 5–10 percent.[2] Taking a mid-value of 7.5 percent, this

---

[2]See Buddin et al. (1992), p. 39; also the survey of pay-elasticity estimates in Warner and Asch (1995), p. 364.

pay increase would boost the Army first-term reenlistment rate from 45 percent to 48.4 percent and the Marine Corps rate from 24 percent to 25.8 percent.

For the Navy, we predicted the effects of capping nonhostile and hostile months for personnel in the highest quintile of nonhostile and hostile months, respectively. The capping policy had a negligible effect on early-career reenlistment, and among first-term personnel, capping nonhostile months also had a negligible effect. But capping hostile months boosted reenlistment from .40 to .43 among the personnel affected. This 7.5-percent increase in reenlistment is about equal to the effect of a 5-percent increase in basic pay, other things constant.

To some extent, higher levels of long or hostile duty might be relieved by deploying those who have not yet had such duty. If so, our results imply that the added duty would increase reenlistment. Yet because personnel are attached to units and develop specialized skills and knowledge about the unit's roles and missions, weaponry/equipment, and fellow unit members, simply swapping one person or unit for another is essentially infeasible. A more subtle means must be devised. If suitable methods to include more personnel cannot be found or are not feasible to implement, the option of using personnel more intensively runs the risks of lower reenlistment and impaired readiness. These potential side effects add to the cost of engaging in peacetime operations.

FURTHER ANALYSIS

It remains for future research to discover whether perstempo in the years following 1995 has affected reenlistment rates. The pace of peacetime operations—with the multiyear involvement in Bosnia, the panoply of humanitarian and disaster-relief efforts, and the necessity of maintaining a higher visibility in the Persian Gulf—has not diminished.

Analysis of the effects of perstempo on personnel is at an early stage. The set of unanswered questions relevant to policy includes:

- Are the effects of long or hostile duty similar for officers?

- Can the effects of foreign postings be distinguished from long or hostile duty coming from military operations?

- Do the effects of long or hostile duty depend on whether one's unit is fully manned and fully equipped?

- How have the level and nature of post–Cold War deployments affected the expectations of youth and new recruits? Is there any evidence of a negative impact on recruiting? Are these new expectations being borne out? And how does the difference between expectations and outcomes affect reenlistment?

- Do the effects of long or hostile duty differ by personnel quality or dependents status, e.g., are high-quality personnel more likely to reenlist?

- How does long or hostile duty affect promotion, and are these effects more important for early-career personnel than first-term personnel?

- Does high perstempo affect stress, morale, and family stability, and have family-support programs been effective in countering these effects, if present?

Improved measures of perstempo, surveys of personnel, and further analysis of existing data, hopefully enriched with new measures, will provide the means to address these questions.

A THEORY OF DEPLOYMENT, PROMOTION, AND RETENTION

■ Theory of Retention

We are interested in the relationship between deployment, professional advancement through promotion, and retention, so we want to place deployment within a model of retention explicitly allowing for promotion. The dynamic theory of retention developed by Asch and Warner (1994), which generalizes the dynamic retention model of Gotz and McCall (1984), provides a good foundation for our analysis. We adapt this model by making the service member's utility depend directly on the extent of deployment and indirectly on the probability of promotion. Deployment is treated as a random variable with known mean and variance. Deployment is first assumed to be exogenous to the individual, and later we discuss the case where it can be affected by the individual.

In the dynamic retention model, the service member maximizes expected future utility. Expected future utility at the start of period t for a service member at grade g is:

$$\tau^m + u^* (d_{gt}) + \delta_g + w_{gt}^m + \beta V_{gt}^* - z(e_{gt})$$

where τ^m is the individual's taste for the military (assumed to be constant), $u^* (d_{gt})$ is the monetary value of the expected utility of deployment, δ_g represents the value of grade-specific nonpecuniary factors other than deployments, w_{gt}^m is the military wage, β is the individual's discount factor, V_{gt}^* is the expected value of future utility at the *end* of period t, and $z(e_{gt})$ denotes the disutility of effort. The model unfolds sequentially. At the beginning of the period the individual decides on actions intended to maximize expected future utility. The actions require effort, and the disutility of effort rises at an increasing rate with the level of effort. The results of the actions are observed at the end of the period. Also observed are two random factors, one related to the individual's deployment outcomes and the second to other random outcomes; both such outcomes are unknowable at the beginning of the period but, having been realized, affect expected future utility as viewed at the end of period t. Given these outcomes, the individual makes a retention decision at the end of period t.

To be more specific, let η_{gt} be the random shock from deployment and ε_{gt} be the random shock from other factors. The expected value of future utility at the end of period t is a weighted sum of the gain from staying in the military, conditional on choosing to stay, and the gain from leaving, with the weights equal to the probability of continuing in service and the probability of leaving, respectively:

$$V_{gt}^* = \Phi_{gt} E(S_{gt} \mid G_{gt}^* + \eta_{gt} + \varepsilon_{gt} > 0) + (1 - \Phi_{gt}) L_{gt} .$$

In this expression, the probability of continuing in the military, Φ_{gt}, equals the product of the probability Φ_{gt}^1 that the military is willing to allow the individual to continue and the probability Φ_{gt}^2 that the individual is willing to continue. The military will permit continuation if the individual's evaluation exceeds the minimum level, i.e., $E_{gt} > E_{gt}^{min}$, and the individual is willing to continue if the gain by staying is positive, i.e., $G_{gt}^* + \eta_{gt} + \varepsilon_{gt} > 0$. Thus:

$$\Phi_{gt} = \Phi_{gt}^1 \Phi_{gt}^2$$

$$\Phi_{gt}^1 = pr(E_{gt} > E_{gt}^{min})$$

$$\Phi_{gt}^2 = pr(G_{gt}^* + \eta_{gt} + \varepsilon_{gt} > 0)$$

where the gain by staying is expressed as the expected return from the strategy of remaining in the military for *at least* another period, minus the gains from leaving immediately, plus the random shocks from deployment and other factors. The unconditional gain from staying is

$$G_{gt}^* = S_{gt} - L_{gt} \text{ where}$$

$$S_{gt} = \pi_{g+1\,t+1}[\tau^m + u^*(d_{g+1\,t+1}) + \delta_{g+1} + w_{g+1\,t+1}^m + \beta V_{g+1\,t+1}^* - z(e_{g+1\,t+1})]$$

$$+ (1 - \pi_{g+1\,t+1})[\tau^m + u^*(d_{gt+1}) + \delta_g + w_{gt+1}^m + \beta V_{gt+1}^* - z(e_{gt+1})]$$

$$L_{gt} = C_{gt} + R_{gt} + \Gamma_t$$

$$\pi_{g+1\,t+1} = \pi(d_{gt} - \mu_d, \alpha, e_{gt}, \alpha_{gt}^{others}, e_{gt}^{others}, \pi_{g+1\,t+1}^*).$$

Because the individual chooses to stay only if the gain by staying is positive, the expected return from the strategy of remaining in the military for *at least* another period, namely $E(S_{gt} \mid G_{gt}^* + \eta_{gt} + \varepsilon_{gt} > 0)$, is larger than the unconditional expected return S_{gt}. Intuitively, the reason for this is that, for any given draw of $\eta_{gt} + \varepsilon_{gt}$, low values of S_{gt} are less likely to result in a high enough $G_{gt}^* = S_{gt} - L_{gt}$ to exceed the stay criterion, $G_{gt}^* + \eta_{g\,t} + \varepsilon_{gt} > 0$. The expected return from remaining in the military for at least one more period is a weighted average of the expected return conditional on promotion to the next grade at the end of period t and the expected return conditional on remaining in the current grade. The terms comprising the expected return in the higher grade parallel those in the current grade: the taste for military service τ^m, the expected utility from deployment $u^*(d_{g+1\,t+1})$, the expected grade-specific amenities δ_{g+1}, the military wage $w_{g+1\,t+1}^m$, and the present value of expected future utility $\beta V_{g+1\,t+1}^*$, minus the disutility of effort $z(e_{g+1\,t+1})$. The expected value from leaving L_{gt} equals the present values of civilian earnings, retirement or separation pay, and nonpecuniary benefits in the civilian sector, or $C_{gt} + R_{gt} + \Gamma_t$. Finally, the probability of promotion depends on the individual's deployments during the period relative to the expected level of deployments

$d_{gt} - \mu_d$, ability α, effort e_{gt}, the abilities and efforts of others, $\alpha_{gt}^{\text{others}}$ and e_{gt}^{others}, and the fraction of personnel the service wants to promote, $\pi_{g+1\,t+1}^{*}$. The asterisk on the latter indicates that this is the individual's expectation of the system-level promotion probability, i.e., the proportion of personnel in grade g in period t who will be promoted to grade g+1 at t+1. We assume the individual's expectation is unbiased, i.e., the individual accurately anticipates the system-level promotion probability.

■ Expected Utility of Deployment

We model the utility of deployment as a function of the utility from deployment itself and the increase or decrease in utility from a level of deployment that differs from the expected level of deployment. As shown below, this is consistent with the idea that when choosing a military occupation, the service member takes into account the expected level of deployment and, at the same time, is not indifferent to the extent to which actual deployment deviates from the expected level. Further, from the individual's perspective looking into the future, the extent of deployment is a random variable. We use these ideas in developing an expression for deployment utility and placing it within the context of the dynamic retention model above.

Ignoring grade and time subscripts for the moment, let μ_d be the expected level of deployment. We use a second-order Taylor expansion that approximates the utility of d deployments:

$$u(d) \simeq u(\mu_d) + u'(d - \mu_d) + \tfrac{1}{2}u''(d - \mu_d)^2.$$

The approximation is general, and it provides a basis for the following quadratic utility function:

$$u(d) = \psi + ax + bx^2 \quad \text{where } \psi = u(\mu_d) \text{ and } x \equiv d - \mu_d.$$

That is, ψ equals the utility of expected deployment, x represents the deviation of actual deployment from expected deployment, and $ax + bx^2$ are the first- and second-order components of deployment utility deriving from the deviation between actual and expected deployment. Also, because the level of deployment d is a random outcome, x is also, and we can relate the deployment shock in the retention model to the deployment draw to as follows:

$$\eta_{gt} \equiv ax + bx^2.$$

This expression is actually a simplification because the right side does not depend on grade level, though generally speaking the utility of deployment can depend on grade level, as the left side suggests.

Although higher-order approximations to the deployment utility function could be used, the second-order approximation seems suitable for our purposes. The second-order approximation allows for the case where deployment utility increases up to some level of deployment and then decreases—too much deployment reduces utility. We recognize that higher-order terms could be added to the approximation, possibly to real advantage. For instance, the addition of higher-order terms would mean that deployment utility is not quadratic; thus, in the case where more deployment eventually reduces utility, in the quadratic form utility must at some point decline absolutely, whereas higher-order terms could lessen the decrease in utility and allow it to increase at a decreasing rate as well as allow for the possibility of (but not compel) an absolute decrease. Also, we will assume deployment follows a normal distribution. We use the normality assumption later when discussing endogenous deployment. Other bell-shaped distributions would result in the same basic insight.

Following the spirit of the dynamic-retention model, the individual wants to maximize expected utility. In this case, the expected utility of deployment is

$$u^* (d_{gt}) \equiv \mathrm{E}(u(d))$$

$$= \psi + \mathrm{E}(ax) + \mathrm{E}(bx^2)$$

$$= \psi + b\, \sigma_d^2.$$

Thus expected utility is a linear function of the utility of expected deployment plus the product of a term reflecting the individual's risk preference and the variance of deployments. We have denoted the expected utility of deployments as for an individual in grade g at the beginning of period t. We assume that the special pays associated with deployment are incorporated into the parameters of the deployment utility function, ψ, a, and b; the pays are received automatically when deployment occurs.

By definition, the individual is risk averse if the expected utility is less than the utility of expected deployments. Since

$$\mathrm{E}(u(d)) - u(\mu_d) = \psi + b\, \sigma_d^2 - (\psi + a(\mu_d - \mu_d) + b(\mu_d - \mu_d)^2)$$

$$= b\, \sigma_d^2$$

it follows that expected utility is less than the utility of expected deployment if and only if $b\, \sigma_d^2 < 0$. Therefore, b must be negative for risk-averse individuals. For such persons a higher variance of deployment reduces expected utility, and the reduction is greater the larger b in absolute value. By comparison, risk preferers' expected utility increases with the variance of deployments.

■ Occupational Choice

At the outset of the military career, nearly all service members have the opportunity to select a military occupation. Although the military has hundreds of occupations, a service member's choice set depends on his or her qualifications, primarily Armed Services Vocational Aptitude Battery (ASVAB) scores, as well as the particular occupations the service wants to fill at that time. In addition, since occupations can differ in the expected level and variance of deployments, each occupation can be characterized by a pair $(\mu_{dj}, \sigma^2_{dj})$, $j = 1, \ldots, J$. Thus, the service member chooses the occupation with the highest expected utility:

$$\text{max} \qquad U_j = \tau^m + \psi_j + b\,\sigma^2_{dj} + \delta_{gj} + w^m_{gt} + \beta V^*_{gtj} - z(e_{gt})$$
$$j, j \in \{\text{offer set}\}$$

Several points are evident. First, individuals will be attracted to occupations where the expected utility of deployments is high in comparison with other occupations. For instance, some persons may be drawn to seagoing occupations because of the utility they place on being deployed at sea; others may be drawn to combat-arms occupations because of the value they place on being deployed near the "action," and others may prefer occupations where deployments are behind the front lines. Others might prefer not to deploy at all in any occupation; for them the expected utility of deployment is negative, but they nevertheless have an incentive to select the occupation with the least disutility from deployment, i.e., the highest utility. Second, persons with a risk aversion to variance in deployments will seek occupations with low variance. Across the services, deployments in the Navy and Marines may be relatively predictable as ship crews rotate between afloat and ashore on a regular basis, but less predictable in the Army, where units may be called up for military operations other than war whose timing and duration are uncertain. To the extent that the service member perceives no difference in the variance of deployments, $b\,\sigma^2_{dj}$ is constant across occupations given the individual's value of b and, like the individual's taste for the military τ^m, has no effect on occupational choice. Third, if the service limits the choice set to a small number of occupations, the individual may be unable to choose the best occupation, let alone the occupation with the expected-utility maximizing level of deployments. However, although the service has an incentive to fill occupations in order to meet immediate occupation-manning requirements, the service also has an incentive to assure a good occupational match with the service member. A good match implies a higher level of expected utility, hence a higher likelihood of retention. Fourth, if an occupation is "unpopular" in the sense that individuals attach low utility to occupation-specific factors, e.g., $\psi_j + b\,\sigma^2_{dj} + \delta_{gj}$, then the service may need to compensate by increasing the expected value of future utility βV^*_{gtj}. For instance, the pace of promotions can be increased or bonuses can be paid. In addition, since βV^*_{gtj} depends not only on future service wages but also on future civilian opportunites, a high value of future civilian opportunities may be sufficient to draw persons into occupations having otherwise unattractive attributes.

In sum, many elements enter a service member's choice of occupation. Because of differences in attributes across occupations (e.g., μ_d) and the differences in preferences across individuals drawn into an occupation, the *average* expected utility can be expected to differ across occupations, and therefore so can the average retention rate.

■ Deployment and Retention

The retention decision is assumed to occur at the end of the period during which the individual might have been deployed. The individual will remain in the military if

$$G^*_{gt} + \eta_{gt} + \varepsilon_{gt} > 0.$$

The expected gains to staying are now conditioned on the realization of deployment, and as mentioned, deployment has a direct effect on utility as well as an indirect effect through promotion. Both random shocks η_{gt} and ε_{gt} represent outcomes bearing on the return to staying in the military for at least another period. In particular, the deployment shock is generated by the military itself, and its impact on the return to staying will be felt by remaining in the military in the next period and avoided by leaving the military. The other random shock represents the net shock of both military-generated and civilian-generated outcomes; the military outcomes will be realized by staying, and the civilian outcomes will be realized by leaving. For deployment, we think of a process where deployment experience in the current period influences the individual's expectations about deployment experience in the next term. This perspective means that the retention decision is not affected because deployment in the current period was greater or less than optimal—even though the individual's utility *during* the current period might therefore have been higher or lower than expected—but because current experience influences expectations about the future. In addition, new enlistees have never experienced deployment, and their actual deployment provides them with information about what aspects they like and dislike. Therefore, their expectations about the level of satisfaction from future deployment will be better informed. (The same kind of interpretation applies to ε_{gt}.) Substituting in for G^*_{gt} we have

$$S_{gt} - L_{gt} + \eta_{gt} + \varepsilon_{gt} > 0$$

$$\pi^x_{g+1\,t+1}[\tau^m + u^*_{g+1\,t+1} + \delta_{g+1} + w^m_{g+1\,t+1} + \beta V^*_{g+1\,t+1} - z(e_{g+1\,t+1})]$$

$$+ (1 - \pi^x_{g+1\,t+1})[\tau^m + u^*_{gt+1} + \delta_g + w^m_{gt+1} + \beta V^*_{gt} - z(e_{gt+1})] - L_{gt}$$

$$+ ax + bx^2 + \varepsilon_{gt} > 0$$

where $\pi^x_{g+1\,t+1}$ is the probability of promotion given the realization of d deployments and hence the particular value of $x = d - \mu_d$, and $ax + bx^2$ indicates the deployment shock.

If on net deployment raises the promotion probability, the gain by staying increases and retention is more likely. The effect of deployment on promotion reflects two aspects of performance that are taken into account in the promotion system. The first concerns factors such as the scope and variety of assignments, duty performance, and awards and decorations, all of which may be enhanced by deployment; there is, however, a downside risk of performing poorly on deployment. The second aspect concerns additional education and training that may be a required for promotion. Deployment might delay education and training and therefore lower the promotion probability. Thus, whether deployment increases the promotion probability is an empirical question.

The effect of realized deployment depends on the individual's preferences for deployment and for the risk of deployment. If an individual would prefer more deployment than expected and then realizes more deployment than expected, the deployment shock is positive and the probability of retention increases. But if the individual would prefer less deployment than expected and then realizes more than expected, the deployment shock is negative and the retention probability decreases. Whether an individual would prefer more or less deployment than expected depends on the individual's preference parameters a and b. For risk-averse individuals, for instance, the term bx^2 will always be negative; this follows because risk aversion implies $b < 0$ and of course $x^2 > 0$. In the following we first assume risk aversion and then assume risk preference.

In general, the effect of x on retention depends on the level of deployment the individual would prefer if he or she were free to choose. This level is the value of x maximizing $ax + bx^2$. For a risk-averse person ($b < 0$) the maximum occurs at $x = -a/2b$. There are two cases to consider. If $a > 0$, an outcome where deployment exceeds the expected level must result in higher utility, provided deployment is not "too high." Maximum utility occurs where $x = -a/2b$, and utility is higher over the range $0 < x < -a/b$. In contrast, if $a < 0$ then the preferred level of deployment is less than the expected level, provided deployment is not "too low." Here, maximum utility again occurs where $x = -a/2b$, which in this case is negative, and utility is higher over the range $-a/b < x < 0$. Thus, depending on preferences, higher-than-expected deployment can increase utility or decrease it, and therefore increase or decrease the likelihood of retention.

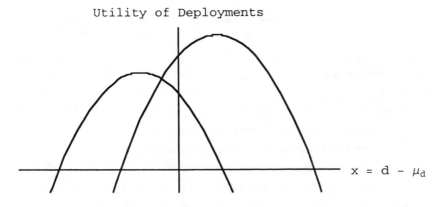

Figure A.1—Heterogeneous Preferences, Risk Aversion

These cases are depicted in Figure A.1 for two persons with different deployment utility functions. For both persons the expected level of deployment occurs where $x = 0$. At this point, the utility of deployment equals ψ since the two other terms of deployment utility drop out, and again ψ represents the utility of expected deployments. The figure is drawn with ψ higher for the person whose maximum utility of deployment occurs above the expected level of deployment. This person would prefer more deployment than the expected level as long as deployment is not too high. Moreover, an outcome of less deployment than expected would definitely reduce this person's utility. In contrast, the person with the lower ψ would prefer less than the expected level of deployment, but not too much less. An outcome of more deployment than expected serves to lower this person's utility.

For risk preferers ($b > 0$), the optimal level of deployment is always higher than the level $x = -a/2b$, which is the point where deployment utility is minimized. If $a > 0$, the minimum occurs where $x < 0$, and as a result, utility must be increasing as x increases through $x = 0$, i.e., where actual deployment equals expected deployment. Consequently, higher-than-expected deployment will increase utility, which is the same result for $a > 0$ as above. Similarly, deployment less than $-a/b$ will also increase utility above the utility of expected deployment. If $a < 0$, then the utility minimum occurs where $x > 0$; hence, utility is decreasing as x increases through $x = 0$. Here, an outcome where deployment is less than expected is preferred, or alternatively, higher than $-a/b$, which is a positive value. The curves in these cases are the upside-down image of the curves in Figure A.1.

Several implications emerge from this analysis. First, if actual deployment equals expected deployment, then there is no deployment shock and hence no "ex post" effect of deployment on retention. Instead, the full effect of deployment works through the term $\psi + b\,\sigma_d^2$, which represents the individual's expected utility of deployment. Other things equal, individuals sort themselves into occupations that provide the highest expected utility, but that is no guarantee that an individual's expected utility of deployment will be positive or that the average expected utility of deployment for personnel in the occupation will be positive.

Second, in order to learn about the relationship between expected deployment and expected utility of deployment, it is necessary to vary the expected level of deployment within an occupation. For instance, by considering a range of increase in expected deployment, variance constant, it would be possible to determine whether a person's expected utility of deployment rose or fell over the range, rose over part of the range and then fell, etc. There is, however, no such variation in the data we use, which are based on deployment from January 1993 through June 1996. This point can be refined by assuming that, after selecting an occupation, individuals are subsequently (after training) assigned to a unit, and units vary in their likelihood of deployment. For instance, the Army organizes itself into branches, and branches differ in deployment rate. Supposing, as seems reasonable, that individuals did not know at the time of selecting an occupation to which particular branch they would be assigned, the actual assignments would create winners and losers. Individuals who preferred a lower expected level of deployment, or less variance, would find themselves better off if assigned to branches with those characteristics (relative to the occupational average across branches). Then, controlling for other possible differences across branches (i.e., nonpecuniary factors δ), it would in principle be possible to determine empirically whether an increase in expected deployment led to an increase in retention and, if so, to infer that the utility of expected deployment ψ rose with expected deployment on average for personnel in the occupation. Similarly, if deployment variance differed across branch, one could estimate the risk parameter b and so infer whether, on average, personnel in the occupation were risk averse with respect to deployment. Such analyses may be possible with future datasets on deployment.

Third, thinking about the model in the context of the four services, it is interesting to contrast the Army and Air Force with the Navy and Marine Corps. Compared to the Navy and Marine Corps, occupations in the Army and Air Force may have a higher deployment variance over our data window, whereas they have substantially lower monthly rates of deployment. Because individuals form expectations and use them in their choice of occupation—and presumably also use them in their choice of service—these differences in the mean and variance of deployment have no necessary relationship to retention rates across services. That is, because of self-selection, the average level of expected deployment *utility*, $\psi + b\,\sigma_d^2$, could be the same across the services despite the underlying differences in mean and variance of deployment. And even if the average level differed, each service could initiate offsetting actions, such as adjusting the promotion rate or applying incentive pays, to raise the average level of expected utility to where expected retention equalled the service's target values. But differences in the variance of deployment can be expected to increase the variance of outcomes among comparable individuals. Higher variance increases the likelihood that actual deployment differs substantially from expected deployment, and therefore the deployment-shock terms $ax + bx^2$ may be larger. For instance, even if risk preference b were the same (on average) across the services, personnel might differ in a, the first-order utility component of a deviation in actual versus expected deployment. For personnel in the Army and Air Force with $a < 0$, deployment above expected levels would reduce utility and so reduce retention. Even if a were the same across services, if the Army and Air Force deployed certain units far more often than expected, then the effect would be more acute and adverse, again assuming $a < 0$. But for personnel for whom $a > 0$, the extra deployment would be welcome and would increase their utility. Thus, it would be completely consistent with the theory and the idea of heterogeneous preferences to have some unit members praise the extra deployment while other unit members complained and left service.

Fourth, the effect of deployment on retention might depend on the service member's marital status and dependency status. For instance, more deployment might be more disruptive to a family than a single person. It might affect the spouse's workload and stress at home, especially if there are young children. Also, many spouses hold jobs, and if home workload and stress increase, there may be spillovers affecting the spouse's performance on the job. Deployed personnel with unaccompanying dependents receive a Family Separation Allowance for deployment at least 30 days long, somewhat offsetting these possible adverse impacts. (Personnel without dependents do not receive a Family Separation Allowance.) Moreover, there are often support groups and support services (e.g., child care, counselors, health care, recreation facilities) on-base that can help families handle extra stress created by deployment. It would be naive, however, not to recognize that service members without dependents nonetheless have close friends and family who may be stressed by the service member's deployment, and the service member may sense this stress and internalize it. Further, the percentage of enlisted personnel and officers who are married rises steadily during the first ten years of service. This means that many single personnel have close relationships, and the effect of deployment on these relationships may be quite similar to the effect felt by married couples. Overall, these factors do not point to an a priori difference in the *net* effect of deployment on retention for single versus married personnel, or personnel with children and other dependents.

Fifth, the model implicitly treats all deployment the same; realistically, however, conditions and experiences may differ among deployments. The most obvious difference is whether the deployment is to a hostile area and is therefore riskier. We can control for hostile versus nonhostile deployment in our empirical work. However, deployment can differ in other ways significant to the individual. The tempo of operations may be extremely high on some deployments, e.g., those involving high levels of alert, round-the-clock movement of materiel, combat operations, or time-urgent delivery of food, medical supplies, and health care. Other deployments may be "slow" or routine. Weather, terrain, insects, disease risk, supportive or nonsupportive local populace, risk of terrorist attack, live fire, threat of bombardment, and so forth also define deployments. Sometimes these factors will be known and expected before the actual deployment—e.g., in a protracted war—but even so, there may be highly stressful realizations during the deployment. These additional dimensions of deployment can be added to the model, and if data quantified the dimensions it would be possible to estimate hedonic specifications showing the average effect of a dimension among the population under study.

■ Endogenous Deployments

Until now we have assumed exogenous deployment. Given that preferences differ and some personnel want more deployment than expected while others want less, however, incentives exist at the individual level to alter the extent of deployment to one's own expected utility-maximizing level. Beyond self-selection into a service and an occupation, discussed above, individuals may have some discretion to increase or decrease their deployment from the expected level. Individuals may be able to volunteer for deployment. For instance, Navy personnel may volunteer for sea duty. The Army fills out deploying task forces by "cross attaching" individuals from various units, and the cross-attaching process may involve an element of individual volunteerism. For many operations other than the largest, an entire unit may not need to deploy as part of a task force, only specific types of personnel. Individuals may have discretion to opt in or opt out of a deployment, provided their unit commander concurs. Similarly, individuals may be able to take actions that increase or reduce their likelihood of deployment. Personnel who like to deploy may "advertise" that they want to be included on any deployment for which they qualify, or they may put in for a transfer to units more likely to deploy. Alternatively, personnel near the end of their term may ask to be excused from a deployment, especially if the deployment does not require the entire unit.

We assume the individual can marginally alter the expected level of deployment and that doing so requires effort. We assume the individual's effort systematically alters the expected level of deployment; that is, we do not treat the relationship between effort and deployment as a stochastic process in which the individual cannot be sure of the outcome. Allowing for randomness in the outcome would reduce the incentive of a risk-averse individual to undertake such effort but otherwise would not change the basic point. The individual, seeking to maximize expected utility, decides at the beginning of period t to exert effort, and the results of the effort are realized by the end of the period, at which time the individual assesses expected future utility and decides to stay or leave.

This problem is essentially the same as Asch and Warner's (1994) analysis of the optimal level of effort to increase expected future utility by increasing the probability of promotion, and we adopt their analysis. The first-order condition for maximizing expected utility is:

$$\frac{\partial U_{gt}}{\partial e_{gt}} = \beta \frac{\partial V_{gt}^*}{\partial e_{gt}} - \frac{\partial z\,(e_{gt})}{\partial e_{gt}} = 0$$

$$= \beta \{ \Phi_{gt} \frac{\partial G_{gt}^*}{\partial e_{gt}} + \Phi_{gt}^2 [E(S_{gt} \mid G_{gt}^* + \eta_{gt} + \epsilon_{gt} > 0) - L_{gt}] \frac{\partial \Phi_{gt}^1}{\partial e_{gt}} \} - \frac{\partial z\,(e_{gt})}{\partial e_{gt}} = 0$$

Optimum effort occurs where the present value of the marginal increase in expected utility equals the marginal disutility of effort. Marginal expected utility has two terms. The first is the probability of continuing in the military at the end of period t, Φ_{gt}, times the change in expected future military versus civilian returns, $G_{gt}^* = S_{gt} - L_{gt}$. The second term represents the effect on the probability of exceeding the minimum standard of performance and being allowed to continue in the military, times the gain in doing so. Specifically, the change in this probability is multiplied by the probability of wanting to continue in service, Φ_{gt}^2, times the expected future utility of military service given that one wants to continue, minus the expected future civilian utility. The last term in the expression is the marginal disutility of effort, i.e., the marginal cost of effort to the individual. In Asch and Warner's analysis of effort, the individual's effort causes an increase in both the probability of promotion and the probability of a successful evaluation (exceeding the minimum), and so the first two terms are unambiguously positive. The situation is less clear in the case of effort to change deployment.

In particular, individuals may choose to increase or decrease deployment and must exert effort either way. As the first-order condition implies, a change in deployment affects utility through promotion, evaluation, and the expected utility from deployment per se. The effect of increased deployment on promotion and evaluation is probably positive—but need not be. Common sense suggests that more deployment will lead to faster promotion for most personnel, but deployment could delay obtaining required training or education. Similarly, deployment has a downside risk. Persons who perform well at their home base may perform less well when deployed, or may face bigger losses from making a mistake. As a result, more deployment does not necessarily increase the chance of a successful evaluation. Second, supposing deployment increases the probability of promotion and successful evaluation, some individuals might nevertheless want to *reduce* their level of deployment. This occurs if the individual's preferred level of deployment is less than the expected level and the direct-utility gains of reducing deployment outweigh the indirect benefits of increasing it, operating through promotion and evaluation. In contrast, persons preferring more deployment would exert effort to increase their deployment opportunities, since they gain both the direct and the indirect effects.

The balance between the promotion effect and the direct utility of deployment can be seen in the explicit form for the partial derivative of G_{gt}^* with respect to e_{gt}:

$$\frac{\partial G_{gt}^*}{\partial e_{gt}} = \frac{\partial (S_{gt} - L_{gt})}{\partial e_{gt}} = \frac{\partial S_{gt}}{\partial e_{gt}}$$

$$= \frac{\partial \pi_{g+1\,t+1}}{\partial e_{gt}} (U_{g+1\,t+1} - U_{gt+1}) + \pi_{g+1\,t+1} \left(\frac{\partial U_{g+1\,t+1}}{\partial e_{gt}} - \frac{\partial U_{gt+1}}{\partial e_{gt}} \right) + \frac{\partial U_{gt+1}}{\partial e_{gt}}$$

The first term on the right side is positive if the effort to change the expected level of deployment causes an increase in the promotion probability. The probability is multiplied by the gain to promotion, i.e., the difference in expected returns in grade g+1 versus g at the beginning of period t+1; this gain is positive. To evaluate the second and third terms, note that

$$\frac{\partial U_{g+1\,t+1}}{\partial e_{gt}} - \frac{\partial U_{gt+1}}{\partial e_{gt}} = \frac{\partial \psi_{g+1\,t+1}}{\partial e_{gt}} - \frac{\partial \psi_{gt+1}}{\partial e_{gt}} \simeq 0$$

$$\frac{\partial U_{gt+1}}{\partial e_{gt}} = \frac{\partial \psi_{gt+1}}{\partial e_{gt}}$$

The term immediately above equals the change in the utility of expected deployments. This term is positive if deployment moves in the direction preferred by the individual, as would happen if there were no other effects. But because of the indirect effects on promotion and evaluation, the individual selects the direction of change in deployment that maximizes overall expected utility, not merely the direct utility from deployment. That is, a person may sign up for more deployment even if he or she does not like deployment per se; the chance of faster promotion or successful evaluation may be the motivating factor. Substituting into the previous expression, we have

$$\frac{\partial G_{gt}^*}{\partial e_{gt}} = \frac{\partial \pi_{g+1\,t+1}}{\partial e_{gt}} (U_{g+1\,t+1} - U_{gt+1}) + \frac{\partial \psi_{gt+1}}{\partial e_{gt}}.$$

In sum, if the individual can change the expected level of deployment, the change may not be in an expected direction. The change may result in higher direct utility from being closer to the preferred level of deployment, or higher indirect utility from improving promotion and evaluation prospects. Either way, effort is required to make a change, and effort will be exerted only if the individual can thereby increase expected future utility. Because expected future utility must increase in order for the effort to be worthwhile, the retention probability at t+1 must also increase. Note, though, that because some individuals may increase their expected deployment while others may reduce theirs, endogenous deployment implies neither a positive correlation or a negative one between deployment and retention. Therefore, self-selected deployment efforts do not necessarily mean that a predictable effect will occur in the regression models of retention as a function of deployment.

The effort that increases the retention probability at t+1 will not necessarily change future retention probabilities. For example, consider a person who plans to leave at the end of a four-year hitch and is now in the second year. Effort to optimize deployment will increase the probability of staying from year two to year three, reducing the probability of attrition. But it may not affect the plan to leave after the fourth year. Still, the probability of staying after the fourth year may increase if, say, deployment optimization in year two led to more rapid promotion, which increased the gain for staying in all future periods, or led to a desirable reassignment that lasted several years and generated opportunities for future desirable assignments.

■ Optempo

With the downsizing of active-duty forces and the increased level of deployment for smaller-scale contingencies (SSCs) that occurred in the early 1990s, the pace of military operations has increased. The services not only must maintain their readiness for a major theater war (MTW), but also must meet the requirements for SSCs and cope with the disruption they create for MTW-readiness activities such as unit training, combined unit training, and inspections. On net, many believe this increase in operating tempo requires greater daily personnel effort. Here, we point out that the model can recognize the increase in optempo by an upward shift in the level of effort demanded; that is, we can think of increased optempo as causing an increase in the level of effort e required. With higher effort as part of the new package, the disutility of effort increases and the expected utility from remaining in the military decreases.

The increase in required effort may differ between deployment and nondeployment, and higher optempo can affect both. For instance, personnel at sea are always on alert, whereas at home port they are not on alert. Deployed logistics personnel must be ready to handle incoming or outgoing cargo around the clock, and deployed medical personnel may have fewer resources in the event of surges in the demand for medical care. To the extent that *expected* optempo is greater during deployment, then the disutility from effort is that much higher. In the model of exogenous deployment, we can introduce this difference by now interpreting d as the proportion of the period spent deployed and $(1 - d)$ as the proportion not deployed, and e_d and e_n as required effort when deployed and not deployed, respectively. The expected disutility of effort at the beginning of period t is therefore $dz(e_{dt}) + (1 - d)z(e_{nt})$. More time deployed along with higher effort during deployment would reduce the individual's expected utility and reduce the probability of reenlistment.

In addition, there is an interaction between the proportion of personnel in a branch and specialty who are deployed and the workload left to be handled by nondeployed personnel. Deploying task forces may draw personnel from many units including some that do not deploy.

The nondeploying units may therefore be shorthanded, but their workload does not necessarily decrease. The remaining personnel may in fact be expected to provide the same level of services as before. This may mean longer hours, weekend duty, and less time for personal and family activities. As a result, the effort of nondeployed unit members may increase, which would decrease their utility and their subsequent retention. This is a testable hypothesis, though not with available data. The required data would indicate the shorthandedness and workload of nondeployed units; the members of shorthanded units with workloads that did not decrease would be expected to have lower retention.

■ Variable Pay

The approach to modeling deployment can be applied to modeling military pay containing a variable component such as bonuses. For instance, a reenlistment bonus can be considered in terms of its expected value and variance, and we can assume the individual is not indifferent to the riskiness of the bonus level. Suppose military pay at the end of period t is $w_{gt} + B_{gt}$, where the bonus has mean $\overline{B}_{gt}$ and variance σ_B^2. The bonus amount depends on military pay at that time. Following the approach for deployments, assume the expected utility of the bonus is $\overline{B}_{gt} + r\,\sigma_B^2$, where r is the risk-preference parameter. The expected return to the strategy of staying in the military at least one more period is:

$$S_{gt} = \pi_{g+1\,t+1}[\tau^m + u^*_{g+1\,t+1} + \delta_{g+1} + w^m_{g+1\,t+1} + \overline{B}_{gt+1} + r\,\sigma_B^2 + \beta V^*_{g+1\,t+1} - z(e_{g+1\,t+1})]$$

$$+ (1 - \pi_{g+1\,t+1})[\tau^m + u^*_{gt+1} + \delta_g + w^m_{gt+1} + \overline{B}_{gt+1} + r\,\sigma_B^2 + \beta V^*_{gt} - z(e_{gt+1})].$$

The presence of the term $r\,\sigma_B^2$ implies that for risk-averse individuals ($r < 0$), the variance of bonuses reduces their expected utility. Further, and possibly more important, to the extent that a given level of pay P shifts from being wholly certain (e.g., $pay = w_{gt}$) to partially certain (e.g., $pay = w'_{gt} + B_{gt}$) but *having the same expected value*, then the expected utility of the pay is reduced:

$$EU(w'_{gt} + B_{gt}) - EU(w_{gt}) = \frac{\overline{B}_{gt}}{w'_{gt} + \overline{B}_{gt}}\, r\,\sigma_B^2 < 0.$$

The decline in expected utility depends on the proportion of pay placed at risk, the size of the variance, and the individual's risk aversion.

The shift to pay with a variable component, holding expected pay constant, may cause a reduction in retention and will cause an increase in expected military pay for those choosing to stay. Expected pay increases because personnel with higher bonuses will be more likely to stay while personnel with lower bonuses will tend to leave, holding other things constant. Two factors affect retention: the risk-aversion term $r\,\sigma_B^2$ and the randomness of the variable component. As mentioned, $r\,\sigma_B^2$ is negative for risk-averse persons, hence it reduces the gain in staying and so reduces retention. The added randomness of the variable component of pay means that the variance of the random shock ε_{gt} has been increased. Notice that this effect would occur even if there were no risk-aversion term. The increase in variance will affect people differently. For personnel with a reenlistment probability above one-half, the increase in variance will tend to reduce the probability, while for personnel with a reenlistment probability below one-half, the increase in variance will tend to increase the probability. Therefore, for risk-averse personnel in the career force, a shift to pay with a variable component would definitely reduce retention. However, for risk-averse personnel in the first term, such a shift might or might not reduce retention, depending on the risk-aversion term compared the variance effect derived below.

Recall that reenlistment requires the gain in staying to be positive: $G_{gt}^* + \varepsilon_{gt} > 0$. Here, ε_{gt} represents all random factors (e.g., it subsumes the random shock of deployment). Assume ε_{gt} is normal with mean μ and variance σ^2. Then the change in the probability of reenlistment with respect to an increase in the variance of ε is

$$\frac{\partial \Pr(\text{reenlistment})}{\partial \sigma} = \frac{\partial \int_{-G^*}^{\infty} F(\varepsilon)\, d\varepsilon}{\partial e_{gt}} = \frac{-(G^* + \mu)}{2\,\sigma^2\,\sqrt{2\,\pi\sigma^2}}\, exp\, \frac{-(G^* + \mu)^2}{2\,\sigma^2}.$$

The derivative is positive if $-(G^* + \mu) > 0$ or equivalently $-G^* > \mu$. When $-G^*$ is less than the mean, the integration over ε begins in the upper half of the distribution and therefore the reenlistment probability is less than .5. For instance, suppose the mean of ε were zero and further suppose G^* were negative because civilian pay was greater than military pay. As a result, $-G^*$ is positive and greater than the mean, and the probability of staying is less than half. Generally, the derivation shows that an increase in the variance of random factors increases the reenlistment probability if the reenlistment probability is initially less than half, and decreases the reenlistment probability if it is initially greater than half. Intuitively, higher variance increases the chance of a good draw if one is in the upper part of the ε distribution, i.e., if integration begins where $-G^* > \mu$, and therefore increases the chance that $G_{gt}^* + \varepsilon_{gt} > 0$, which implies reenlistment. Similarly, a higher variance increases the chance of a bad draw if one is in the lower part of the ε distribution and therefore decreases the chance of reenlistment. Since the first-term reenlistment probability typically lies below half, higher variance in the random factors should tend to increase reenlistment. In contrast, higher variance should tend to reduce career reenlistment, which averages over sixty percent. The effect of increased variance is zero when the reenlistment probability is half. Finally, the larger the increase in variance, the larger the effect, up or down, on the reenlistment probability. When the variable component of pay is small, such as when reenlistment bonuses are low, the reenlistment impact will be small.

STATED INTEREST IN JOINING THE MILITARY

Table B.1 was prepared from tabulations on the 1991 Youth Attitude Tracking Survey (YATS) with 30-month follow-up matching of enlistee records from Military Enlistment Processing Center (MEPCOM) data. Weighted YATS data provide a representative sample of youth, and the match to MEPCOM records allows the identification of sample respondents who subsequently enlisted for active duty in the military services. While the table weights YATS data to reflect the responses of youth in general, the subsequent enlistee data are not weighted. As a result, the enlistee responses are not necessarily representative of the enlistee population.

We chose the 1991 YATS file because of its relevance to first-term personnel making stay/leave decisions about the time covered by our perstempo reenlistment analysis file, i.e., personnel with an expiration of term of service date between July 1995 and June 1996. The percentages shown in the table are fairly typical of other YATS surveys before and since 1991, however. For instance, the patterns seen in the table probably apply to personnel who entered in the late 1980s and who appear in our perstempo file as early careerists.

The responses shown in the table are answers to YATS question Q526, "If you were to consider joining the military, what would be the main reason?" After the respondent answers, the survey administrator asks, "Any other reasons?" but does not give a menu of reasons to choose from. Thus, the respondent may and often does have multiple responses, and responses after the first response are prompted, but not by specific reasons; hence, they can be considered "unaided" mentions.

As the table suggests, reasons such as "away from home," "travel," and "duty to country" may play a role in decisions to enlist. These items are mentioned by both the youth population and the enlistees as reasons for joining the military. Further, long or hostile duty, given the travel and duty involved, may represent a fulfillment of these reasons.

Table B.1

Reasons for Joining the Military: Youth Versus Enlistees
(percent with mention)

Reason	Youth Population	Enlistees
Away from home	2.1	4.3
Retirement benefits	3.3	7.8
Develop discipline	3.9	3.4
Duty to country	15.9	13.8
Pay for education	24.8	27.6
Job training	24.9	43.1
Maturity	0.4	1.7
Would not consider	8.1	2.6
Other	18.2	23.3
Pay	14.9	17.2
Physical challenge	1.5	1.7
Self esteem/pride	3.6	5.2
More structure	1.8	1.7
National defense	2.0	0.9
Teamwork	1.0	1.7
Travel	7.4	13.8

DATA, VARIABLES, REGRESSIONS

DESCRIPTION OF SAMPLE AND VARIABLES

Our reenlistment sample includes service members who: (a) made a reenlistment decision between July 1995 and June 1996, or (b) were eligible to make a reenlistment decision during this time, but made the decision earlier. These groups include people whose original expiration of term of service (ETS) date was during this period, who did not extend, and who made a decision either during this time or before; people whose ETS date was after this period but reenlisted or were discharged during this time; and people who extended their ETS into this period and made a decision during that time. We excluded those who were discharged more than three months early, even if this fell during this period; probably most of these personnel were attritees, not early-outs. (We assume most early-outs are dismissed within three months prior to ETS.) Since we did not have data on their eventual decision, we also excluded people who extended their ETS beyond the follow-up window.

All service members included had to be followed for at least 30 months. Long or hostile duty incidence, months, and episodes variables were derived from the first 24 of the 30 months leading up to their decision.

Table C.1

Variable Means and Standard Deviations: First Term

Variable	Army		Air Force		Navy		Marine Corps	
	Mean	Std. Dev.	Mean	Std. Dev.	Mean	Std. Dev.	Mean	Std. Dev.
Incidence, Months								
Incidence	0.386	0.487	0.307	0.461	0.688	0.463	0.610	0.488
Total months	2.080	0.487	1.511	0.461	5.001	0.463	3.794	0.488
Hostile months	0.587	1.619	0.935	2.380	1.139	1.614	0.540	1.347
Episodes								
None	0.614	0.487	0.693	0.461	0.312	0.463	0.390	0.488
One	0.291	0.454	0.229	0.420	0.231	0.421	0.341	0.474
Two	0.079	0.270	0.059	0.235	0.256	0.436	0.205	0.404
Three or more	0.016	0.124	0.019	0.136	0.202	0.401	0.064	0.245
Hostile Episodes								
None	0.829	0.376	0.780	0.414	0.590	0.492	0.769	0.422
One	0.145	0.352	0.173	0.378	0.351	0.477	0.197	0.398
Two	0.024	0.152	0.035	0.185	0.057	0.231	0.032	0.175
Three or more	0.002	0.044	0.012	0.108	0.003	0.051	0.002	0.048
Other Variables								
AFQT missing	0.019	0.138	0.010	0.101	0.029	0.169	0.006	0.079
AFQT IV and V	0.018	0.134	0.001	0.037	0.007	0.083	0.000	0.016
AFQT IIIB	0.261	0.439	0.138	0.345	0.299	0.458	0.279	0.449
AFQT IIIA	0.291	0.454	0.295	0.456	0.256	0.437	0.300	0.458
AFQT I and II	0.410	0.492	0.556	0.497	0.409	0.492	0.414	0.493
Educ less than HS	0.026	0.159	0.003	0.057	0.021	0.144	0.024	0.152
Educ high school +	0.050	0.218	0.720	0.449	0.026	0.160	0.014	0.118
White	0.709	0.454	0.851	0.356	0.722	0.448	0.779	0.415
Black	0.227	0.419	0.114	0.317	0.173	0.378	0.136	0.343
Hispanic	0.064	0.245	0.035	0.184	0.105	0.307	0.085	0.279
Male	0.873	0.333	0.796	0.403	0.897	0.304	0.964	0.186
Female	0.127	0.333	0.204	0.403	0.103	0.304	0.036	0.186
Infantry etc.	0.241	0.428	0.075	0.263	0.084	0.278	0.348	0.476

Table C.1—continued

Variable	Army		Air Force		Navy		Marine Corps	
	Mean	Std. Dev.	Mean	Std. Dev.	Mean	Std. Dev.	Mean	Std. Dev.
Electronic equipment repairers	0.068	0.251	0.120	0.325	0.086	0.280	0.058	0.235
Communications/ intelligence	0.118	0.322	0.052	0.222	0.150	0.357	0.093	0.291
Medical/dental	0.087	0.282	0.084	0.278	0.099	0.298	0.000	0.000
Other technical	0.025	0.156	0.050	0.218	0.013	0.113	0.019	0.136
Functional support/ administrative	0.135	0.341	0.228	0.420	0.109	0.312	0.136	0.343
Electrical/mechanical repairers	0.174	0.379	0.238	0.426	0.320	0.466	0.157	0.364
Craftsmen	0.031	0.173	0.057	0.231	0.079	0.270	0.033	0.178
Service/supply	0.122	0.328	0.095	0.294	0.060	0.238	0.156	0.363

Table C.2
Variable Means and Standard Deviations: Early Career

Variable	Army		Air Force		Navy		Marine Corps	
	Mean	Std. Dev.	Mean	Std. Dev.	Mean	Std. Dev.	Mean	Std. Dev.
Incidence, Months								
Incidence	0.437	0.496	0.371	0.483	0.473	0.499	0.526	0.499
Total months	2.267	0.496	1.710	0.483	3.040	0.499	2.629	0.499
Hostile months	0.442	1.486	0.816	2.365	0.635	1.357	0.266	1.006
Episodes								
None	0.563	0.496	0.629	0.483	0.527	0.499	0.474	0.499
One	0.301	0.459	0.255	0.436	0.198	0.398	0.330	0.470
Two	0.110	0.313	0.080	0.271	0.161	0.368	0.145	0.352
Three or more	0.026	0.158	0.036	0.187	0.114	0.318	0.051	0.220
Hostile Episodes								
None	0.870	0.336	0.807	0.395	0.767	0.423	0.889	0.315
One	0.112	0.315	0.147	0.354	0.201	0.401	0.098	0.297
Two	0.016	0.124	0.030	0.170	0.029	0.167	0.011	0.106
Three or more	0.002	0.046	0.017	0.128	0.002	0.049	0.002	0.046
Other Variables								
AFQT missing	0.019	0.137	0.029	0.166	0.103	0.304	0.051	0.220
AFQT IV and V	0.160	0.367	0.037	0.190	0.096	0.295	0.071	0.257
AFQT IIIB	0.306	0.461	0.248	0.432	0.227	0.419	0.296	0.456
AFQT IIIA	0.208	0.406	0.242	0.428	0.168	0.374	0.221	0.415
AFQT I and II	0.306	0.461	0.444	0.497	0.406	0.491	0.361	0.480
Educ less than HS	0.048	0.213	0.002	0.040	0.082	0.274	0.071	0.256
Educ high school+	0.130	0.337	0.944	0.230	0.051	0.221	0.054	0.226
White	0.568	0.495	0.776	0.417	0.760	0.427	0.670	0.470
Black	0.377	0.485	0.187	0.390	0.182	0.386	0.267	0.442
Hispanic	0.056	0.229	0.036	0.187	0.058	0.234	0.063	0.244
Male	0.873	0.333	0.852	0.356	0.905	0.294	0.938	0.241
Female	0.127	0.333	0.148	0.356	0.095	0.294	0.062	0.241
Infantry etc.	0.296	0.457	0.068	0.252	0.080	0.271	0.195	0.397

Table C.2—continued

Variable	Army		Air Force		Navy		Marine Corps	
	Mean	Std. Dev.	Mean	Std. Dev.	Mean	Std. Dev.	Mean	Std. Dev.
Electrical equipment repairers	0.061	0.239	0.122	0.328	0.193	0.395	0.085	0.279
Communications/ intelligence	0.097	0.296	0.071	0.257	0.104	0.305	0.092	0.290
Medical/dental	0.072	0.259	0.074	0.262	0.069	0.253	0.000	0.000
Other technical	0.029	0.169	0.036	0.186	0.018	0.134	0.032	0.175
Functional support/ administrative	0.174	0.379	0.252	0.434	0.113	0.317	0.243	0.429
Electrical/mechanical repairers	0.134	0.341	0.258	0.437	0.297	0.457	0.191	0.393
Craftsmen	0.017	0.128	0.045	0.207	0.066	0.248	0.030	0.171
Service/supply	0.119	0.324	0.073	0.261	0.060	0.237	0.131	0.338

Table C.3

Logit Regression of Reenlistment: First Term, Months Specification

Variable	Army		Air Force		Navy		Marine Corps	
	Coef.	Std. Err.	Coef.	Std. Err.	Coef.	Std. Err.	Coef.	Std. Err.
Intercept	−0.977	0.034	−0.144	0.066	−0.589	0.067	−1.800	0.053
Incidence, Months								
Incidence	0.584	0.034	0.070	0.045	0.216	0.051	0.069	0.050
Total months	−0.030	0.004	−0.025	0.007	−0.020	0.005	0.005	0.006
Hostile months	−0.086	0.008	0.007	0.009	−0.053	0.012	−0.033	0.014
Other variables								
AFQT missing	0.116	0.084	0.481	0.164	1.158	0.100	0.400	0.199
AFQT IV and V	0.323	0.085	−0.036	0.399	0.659	0.188	0.723	0.939
AFQT IIIA	0.151	0.031	−0.142	0.047	−0.016	0.042	0.156	0.046
AFQT I and II	0.095	0.030	−0.272	0.045	0.069	0.040	0.128	0.045
Educ less than HS	0.406	0.070	0.168	0.250	0.253	0.106	0.211	0.107
Black	0.663	0.029	0.669	0.050	0.654	0.043	0.545	0.048
Hispanic	0.270	0.046	0.058	0.078	0.129	0.050	0.210	0.060
Female	0.273	0.036	−0.016	0.038	0.051	0.053	0.176	0.085
Electrical equipment repairers	0.276	0.049	0.841	0.067	0.456	0.074	0.620	0.076
Communications/ intelligence	0.156	0.041	0.575	0.081	0.588	0.066	0.531	0.063
Medical/dental	0.646	0.045	0.531	0.073	−0.008	0.075	0.000	
Other technical	0.437	0.074	0.423	0.081	0.763	0.144	1.016	0.116
Functional supprt/ administration	0.800	0.041	0.989	0.061	0.397	0.070	0.879	0.056
Electrical/mechanical repairers	0.051	0.036	0.645	0.059	−0.008	0.060	0.630	0.052
Craftsmen	0.444	0.067	0.378	0.078	−0.039	0.077	0.307	0.102
Service/supply	0.136	0.040	0.153	0.069	0.300	0.082	0.372	0.055

Table C.3—continued

Variable	Army		Air Force		Navy		Marine Corps	
	Coef.	Std. Err.	Coef.	Std. Err.	Coef.	Std. Err.	Coef.	Std. Err.
Number of observations	34,589		21,086		18,213		19,726	
–2ln likelihood[a]	47,187	45,130	28,662	27,891	25,061	24,281	22,029	21,424
Chi square; p value	2057	0.0001	771	0.0001	780	0.0001	605	0.0001

[a]For each regression, the first entry for –2ln likelihood is the value with intercept only, and the second entry is the value with all explanatory variables.

Table C.4

Logit Regression of Reenlistment: Early Career, Months Specification

Variable	Army		Air Force		Navy		Marine Corps	
	Coef.	Std. err.	Coef.	Std. err.	Coef.	Std. err.	Coef.	Std. err.
Intercept	1.119	0.030	0.912	0.051	1.060	0.050	0.575	0.072
Incidence, Months								
Incidence	0.461	0.030	0.458	0.033	0.320	0.038	0.469	0.064
Total months	−0.035	0.004	−0.006	0.005	−0.005	0.005	−0.019	0.009
Hostile months	−0.030	0.007	−0.016	0.007	−0.011	0.011	−0.029	0.024
Other Variables								
AFQT missing	0.124	0.081	0.178	0.076	0.373	0.048	0.520	0.126
AFQT IV and V	0.454	0.036	0.348	0.072	0.203	0.048	0.647	0.114
AFQT IIIA	−0.115	0.030	−0.076	0.033	−0.061	0.038	−0.043	0.067
AFQT I and II	0.087	0.029	−0.039	0.031	−0.391	0.032	−0.077	0.062
Educ less than HS	−0.269	0.048	−0.493	0.263	0.145	0.044	0.009	0.091
Black	0.233	0.026	0.255	0.033	0.007	0.033	0.121	0.059
Hispanic	0.198	0.050	0.134	0.064	−0.178	0.048	0.120	0.100
Female	0.017	0.034	−0.416	0.033	−0.170	0.040	−0.193	0.099
Electronic equipment repairers	−0.523	0.046	−0.008	0.056	−0.250	0.050	0.195	0.097
Communications/ intelligence	−0.134	0.041	0.146	0.064	0.075	0.056	0.288	0.095
Medical/dental	−0.462	0.044	0.327	0.064	−0.057	0.061	0.000	
Other technical	0.202	0.073	0.023	0.076	0.378	0.103	0.603	0.154
Functional support/ administrative	−0.096	0.035	0.044	0.051	0.386	0.058	0.374	0.075
Electrical/mechanical repairers	−0.440	0.035	−0.057	0.050	−0.341	0.047	0.243	0.075
Craftsmen	−0.549	0.080	−0.059	0.070	0.084	0.064	−0.092	0.139
Service/supply	−0.446	0.036	0.052	0.062	0.017	0.065	0.043	0.083

Table C.4—continued

Variable	Army		Air Force		Navy		Marine Corps	
	Coef.	Std. err.	Coef.	Std. err.	Coef.	Std. err.	Coef.	Std. err.
Number of observations	48,909		39,457		39,142		9475	
−2ln likelihood[a]	53,988	52,858	45,262	44,652	46,478	45,301	11,016	10,833
Chi square; p value	1130	0.0001	611	0.0001	1177	0.0001	183	0.0001

[a]For each regression, the first entry for −2ln likelihood is the value with intercept only, and the second entry is the value with all explanatory variables.

Table C.5

Logit Regression of Reenlistment: First Term, Episodes Specification

Variable	Army		Air Force		Navy		Marine Corps	
	Coef.	Std. err.	Coef.	Std. err.	Coef.	Std. err.	Coef.	Std. err.
Intercept	-0.971	0.034	-0.155	0.066	-0.594	0.068	-1.788	0.053
Episodes								
One	0.436	0.029	0.117	0.053	0.178	0.047	0.168	0.043
Two	0.644	0.050	0.103	0.096	0.176	0.050	0.123	0.053
Three +	0.906	0.102	0.093	0.179	0.061	0.054	0.133	0.081
Hostile Episodes								
One	-0.370	0.038	-0.218	0.060	-0.290	0.039	-0.192	0.048
Two	-1.019	0.090	-0.157	0.118	-0.107	0.073	-0.407	0.115
Three +	-0.928	0.278	-0.097	0.220	-0.099	0.299	-0.361	0.383
Other Variables								
AFQT missing	0.104	0.084	0.481	0.163	1.141	0.100	0.406	0.200
AFQT IV and V	0.313	0.085	-0.040	0.399	0.652	0.188	0.843	0.935
AFQT IIIA	0.150	0.031	-0.140	0.047	-0.017	0.042	0.154	0.046
AFQT I and II	0.095	0.030	-0.271	0.045	0.069	0.040	0.125	0.045
Educ less than HS	0.392	0.070	0.161	0.250	0.255	0.106	0.218	0.107
Black	0.656	0.029	0.665	0.050	0.659	0.043	0.544	0.048
Hispanic	0.264	0.046	0.057	0.078	0.127	0.050	0.210	0.060
Female	0.273	0.036	-0.017	0.038	0.054	0.053	0.174	0.085
Electrical equipment repairers	0.258	0.049	0.851	0.067	0.470	0.074	0.607	0.076
Communications/ Intelligence	0.144	0.041	0.584	0.081	0.590	0.066	0.529	0.063
Medical/dental	0.650	0.045	0.538	0.073	0.001	0.075	0.000	
Other technical	0.447	0.074	0.437	0.081	0.776	0.145	0.997	0.116
Functional support/ administrative	0.791	0.041	1.000	0.061	0.401	0.070	0.865	0.056
Electrical/mechanical repairers	0.040	0.036	0.661	0.059	-0.001	0.060	0.621	0.052
Craftsmen	0.489	0.067	0.391	0.078	-0.065	0.077	0.290	0.102
Service/supply	0.136	0.040	0.165	0.068	0.308	0.082	0.358	0.055

Table C.5—continued

Variable	Army		Air Force		Navy		Marine Corps	
	Coef.	Std. err.	Coef.	Std. err.	Coef.	Std. err.	Coef.	Std. err.
Number of observations	34,589		21,086		18,213		19,726	
−2ln likelihood[a]	47,187	45,114	28,662	27,890	25,061	24,264	22,029	21,399
Chi square; p value	2072	0.0001	772	0.0001	796	0.0001	630	0.0001

[a]For each regression, the first entry for −2ln likelihood is the value with intercept only, and the second entry is the value with all explanatory variables.

Table C.6
Logit Regression of Reenlistment: Early Career, Episodes Specification

Variable	Army Coef.	Army Std. err.	Air Force Coef.	Air Force Std. err.	Navy Coef.	Navy Std. err.	Marine Corps Coef.	Marine Corps Std. err.
Intercept	1.118	0.030	0.905	0.051	1.061	0.050	0.555	0.073
Episodes								
One	0.313	0.027	0.487	0.036	0.311	0.034	0.288	0.055
Two	0.309	0.040	0.602	0.058	0.297	0.038	0.565	0.080
Three +	0.786	0.085	0.962	0.107	0.329	0.044	0.792	0.130
Hostile Episodes								
One	-0.286	0.038	-0.277	0.043	-0.093	0.036	-0.179	0.086
Two	-0.466	0.089	-0.269	0.089	0.000	0.076	-0.282	0.236
Three +	-0.372	0.264	-0.542	0.144	0.111	0.262	-1.178	0.476
Other Variables								
AFQT missing	0.120	0.081	0.176	0.076	0.373	0.048	0.526	0.126
AFQT IV and V	0.452	0.036	0.347	0.072	0.203	0.048	0.646	0.114
AFQT IIIA	-0.114	0.030	-0.075	0.033	-0.062	0.038	-0.034	0.067
AFQT I and II	0.089	0.029	-0.039	0.031	-0.392	0.032	-0.079	0.062
Educ less than HS	-0.268	0.048	-0.491	0.263	0.146	0.044	0.004	0.091
Black	0.226	0.026	0.250	0.033	0.007	0.033	0.118	0.059
Hispanic	0.194	0.050	0.128	0.064	-0.179	0.048	0.113	0.100
Female	0.011	0.034	-0.412	0.033	-0.170	0.040	-0.185	0.099
Electrical equipment repairers	-0.518	0.046	-0.005	0.057	-0.252	0.050	0.206	0.098
Communications/ intelligence	-0.128	0.041	0.150	0.064	0.073	0.056	0.306	0.095
Medical/dental	-0.458	0.044	0.331	0.065	-0.057	0.061	0.000	0.061
Other technical	0.208	0.073	0.033	0.076	0.378	0.103	0.628	0.154
Functional support/ administration	-0.093	0.035	0.054	0.052	0.385	0.058	0.409	0.075
Electrical/mechanical repairers	-0.440	0.035	-0.048	0.051	-0.341	0.047	0.251	0.076
Craftsmen	-0.497	0.080	-0.053	0.071	0.080	0.064	-0.057	0.139
Service/supply	-0.435	0.036	0.063	0.063	0.017	0.065	0.066	0.083

Table C.6—continued

Variable	Army		Air Force		Navy		Marine Corps	
	Coef.	Std. err.	Coef.	Std. err.	Coef.	Std. err.	Coef.	Std. err.
Number of observations	48,909		39,457		39,142		9475	
–2ln likelihood[a]	53,988	52,884	45,262	44,602	46,478	45,296	11,016	10,814
Chi square; p value	1104	0.0001	660	0.0001	1182	0.0001	203	0.0001

[a]For each regression, the first entry for –2ln likelihood is the value with intercept only, and the second entry is the value with all explanatory variables.

DEPENDENTS STATUS TABLES AND REGRESSIONS

This appendix contains several items: the means and standard deviations of pers-tempo variables conditional on dependents status, sets of regressions incorporating these variables, and tables of the difference between perstempo coefficients for persons with and those without dependents and the statistical significance of those differences. Means and standard deviations for variables other than perstempo variables are given in Tables C.1 and C.2 and therefore are not repeated here. Throughout the appendix, dependents status is defined as of the month of the person's reenlistment decision.

Table D.1

Perstempo Means and Standard Deviations by Dependents Status: First Term

Variable	Army Mean	Army Std. dev.	Air Force Mean	Air Force Std. dev.	Navy Mean	Navy Std. dev.	Marine Corps Mean	Marine Corps Std. dev.
No Dependents								
Incidence, Months								
Incidence	0.380	0.485	0.338	0.473	0.720	0.449	0.536	0.499
Total months	2.217	0.485	1.950	0.473	5.372	0.449	3.050	0.499
Hostile months	0.694	1.756	1.224	2.689	1.259	1.668	0.634	1.553
Episodes								
None	0.620	0.485	0.662	0.473	0.280	0.449	0.464	0.499
One	0.295	0.456	0.249	0.433	0.201	0.401	0.308	0.462
Two	0.072	0.259	0.070	0.254	0.271	0.444	0.185	0.389
Three +	0.013	0.114	0.019	0.135	0.248	0.432	0.043	0.203
Hostile Episodes								
None	0.803	0.398	0.728	0.445	0.552	0.497	0.743	0.437
One	0.165	0.371	0.208	0.406	0.382	0.486	0.215	0.411
Two	0.030	0.171	0.050	0.217	0.063	0.242	0.040	0.195
Three +	0.002	0.045	0.015	0.122	0.004	0.060	0.003	0.052
Dependents								
Incidence, Months								
Incidence	0.391	0.488	0.284	0.451	0.658	0.474	0.680	0.466
Total months	1.973	0.488	1.183	0.451	4.653	0.474	4.500	0.466
Hostile months	0.503	1.498	0.720	2.095	1.027	1.554	0.451	1.109
Episodes								
None	0.609	0.488	0.716	0.451	0.342	0.474	0.320	0.466
One	0.288	0.453	0.214	0.410	0.258	0.438	0.372	0.483
Two	0.085	0.279	0.051	0.219	0.242	0.428	0.223	0.417
Three +	0.017	0.131	0.019	0.136	0.158	0.365	0.084	0.278

Table D.1—continued

Variable	Army		Air Force		Navy		Marine Corps	
	Mean	Std. dev.	Mean	Std. dev.	Mean	Std. dev.	Mean	Std. dev.
Hostile episodes								
None	0.850	0.357	0.819	0.385	0.625	0.484	0.793	0.405
One	0.130	0.336	0.147	0.354	0.322	0.467	0.181	0.385
Two	0.019	0.135	0.025	0.156	0.051	0.220	0.024	0.153
Three +	0.002	0.043	0.010	0.097	0.002	0.041	0.002	0.044

Table D.2

Perstempo Means and Standard Deviations by Dependents Status: Early Career

Variable	Army		Air Force		Navy		Marine Corps	
	Mean	Std. dev.	Mean	Std. dev.	Mean	Std. dev.	Mean	Std. dev.
No Dependents								
Incidence, Months								
Incidence	0.378	0.485	0.356	0.479	0.537	0.499	0.326	0.469
Total months	2.371	0.485	2.229	0.479	3.520	0.499	1.636	0.469
Hostile months	0.578	1.681	1.166	2.822	0.771	1.518	0.403	1.317
Episodes								
None	0.622	0.485	0.644	0.479	0.463	0.499	0.674	0.469
One	0.288	0.453	0.259	0.438	0.191	0.393	0.219	0.414
Two	0.077	0.267	0.064	0.246	0.187	0.390	0.083	0.276
Three +	0.013	0.111	0.033	0.179	0.159	0.366	0.024	0.153
Hostile Episodes								
None	0.840	0.367	0.747	0.435	0.731	0.444	0.847	0.361
One	0.135	0.342	0.182	0.386	0.230	0.421	0.125	0.331
Two	0.023	0.151	0.044	0.205	0.035	0.184	0.025	0.156
Three +	0.002	0.044	0.027	0.161	0.004	0.063	0.004	0.061
Dependents								
Incidence, Months								
Incidence	0.444	0.497	0.373	0.484	0.459	0.498	0.552	0.497
Total months	2.255	0.497	1.631	0.484	2.938	0.498	2.757	0.497
Hostile months	0.426	1.460	0.763	2.284	0.606	1.319	0.248	0.957
Episodes								
None	0.556	0.497	0.627	0.484	0.541	0.498	0.448	0.497
One	0.303	0.459	0.254	0.435	0.199	0.399	0.345	0.475
Two	0.114	0.317	0.082	0.274	0.156	0.362	0.153	0.360
Three +	0.027	0.163	0.037	0.188	0.104	0.306	0.054	0.226
Hostile episodes								
None	0.874	0.332	0.816	0.388	0.775	0.417	0.894	0.308
One	0.109	0.312	0.142	0.349	0.195	0.396	0.094	0.292
Two	0.015	0.121	0.027	0.163	0.027	0.163	0.010	0.098
Three+	0.002	0.047	0.015	0.122	0.002	0.046	0.002	0.044

Table D.2—continued

Variable	Army		Air Force		Navy		Marine Corps	
	Mean	Std. dev.	Mean	Std. dev.	Mean	Std. dev.	Mean	Std. dev.
Hostile Episodes								
None	0.874	0.332	0.816	0.388	0.775	0.417	0.894	0.308
One	0.109	0.312	0.142	0.349	0.195	0.396	0.094	0.292
Two	0.015	0.121	0.027	0.163	0.027	0.163	0.010	0.098
Three +	0.002	0.047	0.015	0.122	0.002	0.046	0.002	0.044

Table D.3

Logit Regression of Reenlistment: First Term, Months Specification, Dependents Status

Variable	Army		Air Force		Navy		Marine Corps	
	Mean	Std. dev.	Mean	Std. dev.	Mean	Std. dev.	Mean	Std. dev.
Intercept	−1.244	0.038	−0.377	0.069	−0.817	0.075	−1.898	0.058
No Dependents								
Incidence	0.405	0.057	−0.025	0.070	0.264	0.077	−0.258	0.086
Total months	−0.029	0.007	−0.015	0.010	−0.053	0.008	0.003	0.012
Hostile months	−0.058	0.012	0.015	0.012	−0.027	0.017	0.043	0.018
Having Dependents	0.556	0.030	0.393	0.035	0.513	0.056	0.476	0.053
Incidence	0.595	0.043	0.081	0.059	0.187	0.068	0.130	0.063
Total months	−0.020	0.005	−0.019	0.012	0.012	0.007	−0.011	0.006
Hostile months	−0.079	0.011	0.010	0.014	−0.056	0.016	−0.049	0.022
Other Variables								
AFQT missing	0.134	0.085	0.461	0.164	1.070	0.101	0.376	0.201
AFQT IV and V	0.293	0.086	−0.014	0.400	0.608	0.191	0.968	0.939
AFQT IIIA	0.161	0.031	−0.145	0.048	−0.014	0.043	0.147	0.046
AFQT I and II	0.108	0.031	−0.271	0.045	0.080	0.040	0.130	0.045
Educ less than HS	0.323	0.070	0.110	0.251	0.121	0.108	0.130	0.108
Black	0.654	0.029	0.698	0.050	0.610	0.044	0.534	0.048
Hispanic	0.258	0.047	0.053	0.078	0.081	0.051	0.199	0.060
Female	0.222	0.036	−0.057	0.039	0.008	0.054	0.070	0.086
Electrical equipment repairers	0.203	0.050	0.853	0.068	0.398	0.076	0.477	0.077
Communications/ intelligence	0.135	0.041	0.582	0.082	0.589	0.067	0.436	0.064
Medical/dental	0.561	0.046	0.541	0.073	−0.081	0.076	0.000	
Other technical	0.392	0.074	0.422	0.081	0.743	0.146	0.881	0.117
Functional support/ administration	0.736	0.041	1.007	0.062	0.358	0.072	0.759	0.057
Electrical/mechanical repairers	−0.014	0.037	0.658	0.060	−0.044	0.061	0.535	0.053
Craftsmen	0.345	0.068	0.380	0.079	−0.122	0.078	0.164	0.103
Service/supply	0.075	0.041	0.164	0.069	0.228	0.083	0.243	0.056

Table D.3—continued

Variable	Army		Air Force		Navy		Marine Corps	
	Mean	Std. dev.	Mean	Std. dev.	Mean	Std. dev.	Mean	Std. dev.
Number of observations	34,589		21,086		18,213		19,726	
–2ln likelihood[a]	47,187	44,350	28,662	27,689	25,061	23,634	22,029	21,118
Chi square; p value	2836	0.0001	973	0.0001	1427	0.0001	911	0.0001

[a]For each regression, the first entry for –2ln likelihood is the value with intercept only, and the second entry is the value with all explanatory variables.

Table D.4

Logit Regression of Reenlistment: Early Career, Months Specification, Dependents Status

Variable	Army Mean	Army Std. dev.	Air Force Mean	Air Force Std. dev.	Navy Mean	Navy Std. dev.	Marine Corps Mean	Marine Corps Std. dev.
Intercept	0.610	0.046	0.682	0.062	0.480	0.060	0.269	0.102
No Dependents								
Incidence	-0.032	0.091	0.273	0.094	0.075	0.076	-0.076	0.202
Total months	-0.013	0.010	0.012	0.012	-0.015	0.010	0.018	0.031
Hostile months	0.000	0.019	-0.018	0.014	0.014	0.020	-0.068	0.055
Having Dependents	0.576	0.040	0.257	0.040	0.654	0.040	0.352	0.086
Incidence	0.480	0.032	0.468	0.035	0.422	0.044	0.486	0.068
Total months	-0.034	0.004	-0.006	0.006	0.002	0.006	-0.025	0.009
Hostile months	-0.024	0.008	-0.013	0.008	-0.012	0.013	0.009	0.028
Other Variables								
AFQT missing	0.127	0.082	0.179	0.076	0.351	0.049	0.529	0.127
AFQT IV and V	0.415	0.037	0.336	0.072	0.174	0.048	0.631	0.114
AFQT IIIA	-0.098	0.030	-0.069	0.033	-0.044	0.039	-0.023	0.067
AFQT I and II	0.111	0.029	-0.029	0.031	-0.340	0.033	-0.051	0.063
Educ less than HS	-0.301	0.048	-0.506	0.263	0.086	0.044	-0.007	0.092
Black	0.240	0.026	0.262	0.033	0.000	0.034	0.130	0.059
Hispanic	0.181	0.050	0.133	0.064	-0.176	0.049	0.113	0.101
Female	0.048	0.035	-0.401	0.033	-0.136	0.041	-0.177	0.099
Electrical equipment repairers	-0.520	0.046	-0.007	0.056	-0.198	0.051	0.179	0.098
Communications/intelligence	-0.130	0.041	0.150	0.064	0.084	0.057	0.294	0.096
Medical/dental	-0.464	0.044	0.322	0.064	-0.046	0.062	0.000	
Other technical	0.214	0.073	0.019	0.076	0.397	0.104	0.610	0.154
Functional support/administration	-0.100	0.036	0.045	0.052	0.397	0.058	0.368	0.075
Electrical/mechanical repairers	-0.445	0.035	-0.060	0.050	-0.324	0.047	0.249	0.076
Craftsmen	-0.555	0.080	-0.061	0.071	0.069	0.064	-0.103	0.139
Service/supply	-0.445	0.037	0.051	0.062	0.027	0.066	0.037	0.083

Table D.4—continued

Variable	Army		Air Force		Navy		Marine Corps	
	Mean	Std. dev.	Mean	Std. dev.	Mean	Std. dev.	Mean	Std. dev.
Number of observations	48,909		39,457		39,142		9475	
–2ln likelihood[a]	53,988	52,334	45,262	44,571	46,478	44,324	11,016	10,772
Chi square; p value	1654	0.0001	691	0.0001	2153	0.0001	244	0.0001

[a]For each regression, the first entry for –2ln likelihood is the value with intercept only, and the second entry is the value with all explanatory variables.

Table D.5
Logit Regression of Reenlistment: First Term, Episodes Specification, Dependents Status

Variable	Army Mean	Army Std. dev.	Air Force Mean	Air Force Std. dev.	Navy Mean	Navy Std. dev.	Marine Corps Mean	Marine Corps Std. dev.
Intercept	-1.238	0.038	-0.381	0.069	-0.830	0.075	-1.894	0.058
No Dependents								
Episodes								
One	0.200	0.048	0.037	0.090	0.091	0.072	-0.074	0.073
Two	0.385	0.088	0.106	0.166	0.028	0.072	-0.270	0.092
Three +	0.928	0.174	-0.161	0.378	-0.104	0.077	-0.295	0.163
Hostile Episodes								
One	-0.138	0.060	-0.136	0.097	-0.299	0.058	-0.071	0.081
Two	-0.782	0.138	-0.122	0.189	-0.142	0.105	-0.071	0.167
Three +	-1.653	0.521	0.180	0.416	0.053	0.373	0.291	0.525
Having Dependents	0.556	0.030	0.393	0.035	0.514	0.056	0.476	0.053
Episodes								
One	0.336	0.061	0.082	0.112	0.114	0.093	0.161	0.090
Two	0.248	0.107	-0.115	0.203	0.348	0.097	0.324	0.111
Three +	-0.219	0.215	0.100	0.432	0.539	0.107	0.249	0.187
Hostile Episodes								
One	-0.247	0.078	-0.001	0.125	0.043	0.080	-0.012	0.103
Two	-0.117	0.186	0.210	0.250	0.045	0.150	-0.218	0.235
Three +	1.329	0.634	-0.048	0.503	-0.159	0.647	-0.800	0.776
Other Variables								
AFQT missing	0.125	0.085	0.462	0.164	1.074	0.101	0.374	0.201
AFQT IV and V	0.287	0.086	-0.022	0.400	0.600	0.191	1.061	0.942
AFQT IIIA	0.160	0.031	-0.144	0.048	-0.015	0.043	0.145	0.046
AFQT I and II	0.109	0.031	-0.270	0.045	0.081	0.040	0.127	0.046
Educ less than HS	0.314	0.070	0.102	0.251	0.126	0.108	0.139	0.108
Black	0.648	0.029	0.695	0.050	0.615	0.044	0.529	0.048
Hispanic	0.254	0.047	0.053	0.078	0.084	0.051	0.196	0.060
Female	0.221	0.036	-0.058	0.039	0.012	0.054	0.073	0.086
Electrical equipment repairers	0.186	0.050	0.856	0.068	0.410	0.076	0.480	0.077

Table D.5—continued

Variable	Army		Air Force		Navy		Marine Corps	
	Mean	Std. dev.	Mean	Std. dev.	Mean	Std. dev.	Mean	Std. dev.
Communications/ intelligence	0.125	0.041	0.584	0.081	0.588	0.067	0.442	0.064
Medical/dental	0.562	0.046	0.542	0.073	-0.051	0.076	0.000	
Other technical	0.398	0.074	0.427	0.081	0.774	0.147	0.875	0.117
Functional support/ administrative	0.728	0.041	1.011	0.062	0.362	0.072	0.757	0.057
Electrical/mechanical repairers	-0.024	0.037	0.663	0.060	0.037	0.061	0.534	0.053
Craftsmen	0.381	0.068	0.385	0.079	-0.145	0.078	0.165	0.103
Service/supply	0.075	0.041	0.168	0.069	0.237	0.083	0.239	0.056
Number of observations	34,589		21,086		8213		19726	
-2ln likelihood[a]	47,187	44,325	28,662	27,687	25,061	23,633	22,029	21,116
Chi square; p value	2862	0.0001	975	0.0001	1427	0.0001	913	0.0001

[a]For each regression, the first entry for −2ln likelihood is the value with intercept only, and the second entry is the value with all explanatory variables.

Table D.6

Logit Regression of Reenlistment: Early Career, Episodes Specification, Dependents Status

Variable	Army Mean	Army Std. dev.	Air Force Mean	Air Force Std. dev.	Navy Mean	Navy Std. dev.	Marine Corps Mean	Marine Corps Std. dev.
Intercept	0.609	0.046	0.672	0.062	0.482	0.060	0.248	0.102
No Dependents								
Episodes								
One	-0.097	0.075	0.429	0.109	0.216	0.074	-0.014	0.190
Two	-0.214	0.130	0.720	0.236	-0.115	0.077	0.150	0.270
Three +	0.356	0.304	0.825	0.441	-0.127	0.084	0.174	0.472
Hostile Episodes								
One	-0.022	0.099	-0.251	0.124	-0.013	0.071	-0.208	0.235
Two	0.060	0.222	-0.572	0.270	0.060	0.143	-0.218	0.461
Three +	-0.815	0.708	-0.359	0.482	0.069	0.404	-0.779	1.106
Having Dependents	0.576	0.040	0.257	0.040	0.653	0.040	0.353	0.086
Episodes								
One	0.448	0.080	0.057	0.115	0.144	0.083	0.288	0.198
Two	0.520	0.137	-0.153	0.243	0.622	0.089	0.378	0.283
Three +	0.388	0.317	0.075	0.455	0.768	0.099	0.569	0.490
Hostile Episodes								
One	-0.239	0.107	0.000	0.133	-0.112	0.082	0.130	0.253
Two	-0.477	0.243	0.432	0.288	-0.107	0.172	0.221	0.548
Three +	0.630	0.768	-0.101	0.507	0.271	0.556	-0.286	1.228
Other Variables								
AFQT missing	0.123	0.082	0.177	0.076	0.351	0.049	0.534	0.127
AFQT IV and V	0.414	0.037	0.336	0.072	0.173	0.048	0.631	0.114
AFQT IIIA	-0.098	0.030	-0.069	0.033	-0.043	0.039	-0.013	0.067
AFQT I and II	0.113	0.029	-0.030	0.031	-0.342	0.033	-0.051	0.063
Educ less than HS	-0.301	0.048	-0.503	0.263	0.087	0.044	-0.013	0.092
Black	0.234	0.026	0.259	0.033	0.002	0.034	0.128	0.059
Hispanic	0.177	0.050	0.128	0.064	-0.178	0.049	0.109	0.101
Female	0.043	0.035	-0.399	0.033	-0.140	0.041	-0.169	0.099
Electrical equipment repairers	-0.516	0.046	0.000	0.057	-0.202	0.051	0.193	0.098

Table D.6—continued

Variable	Army		Air Force		Navy		Marine Corps	
	Mean	Std. dev.	Mean	Std. dev.	Mean	Std. dev.	Mean	Std. dev.
Communications/ intelligence	-0.126	0.041	0.157	0.064	0.081	0.057	0.305	0.096
Medical/dental	-0.461	0.044	0.330	0.065	-0.043	0.062	0.000	
Other technical	0.217	0.073	0.033	0.076	0.396	0.104	0.630	0.154
Functional support/ administrative	-0.097	0.036	0.059	0.052	0.395	0.058	0.402	0.076
Electrical/mechanical repairers	-0.446	0.035	-0.048	0.051	-0.325	0.047	0.257	0.076
Craftsmen	-0.511	0.080	-0.049	0.071	0.068	0.064	-0.063	0.139
Service/supply	-0.437	0.037	0.066	0.063	0.023	0.066	0.060	0.083
Number of observations	48,909		39,457		39,142		9475	
-2ln likelihood[a]	53,988	52,355	45,262	44,528	46,478	44,269	11,016	10,759
Chi square; p value	1633	0.0001	734	0.0001	2209	0.0001	257	0.0001

[a]For each regression, the first entry for -2ln likelihood is the value with intercept only, and the second entry is the value with all explanatory variables.

Table D.7

Perstempo Coefficient Difference: Months and Episodes Regressions, First Term

Variable	Army		Air Force		Navy		Marine Corps	
	Diff.	P value	Diff.	P value	Diff.	P value	Diff.	P value
Incidence, Months								
Incidence	0.190	0.007	0.106	0.247	−0.078	0.443	0.389	0.000
Total months	0.009	0.305	−0.005	0.752	0.065	0.000	−0.014	0.308
Hostile months	−0.021	0.213	−0.005	0.762	−0.029	0.217	−0.092	0.002
Episodes								
One	0.336	0.000	0.082	0.465	0.114	0.221	0.161	0.074
Two	0.248	0.021	−0.115	0.571	0.348	0.000	0.324	0.004
Three +	−0.219	0.309	0.100	0.818	0.539	0.000	0.249	0.183
Hostile Episodes								
One	−0.247	0.002	−0.001	0.993	0.043	0.589	−0.012	0.906
Two	−0.117	0.530	0.210	0.400	0.045	0.766	−0.218	0.353
Three +	1.329	0.036	−0.048	0.924	−0.159	0.806	−0.800	0.303

NOTE: Diff. = coefficient for personnel with dependents minus coefficient for personnel without dependents; P value = significance level for rejecting the hypothesis that the difference equals zero.

Table D.8

Perstempo Coefficient Difference: Months and Episodes Regressions, Early Career

Variable	Army		Air Force		Navy		Marine Corps	
	Diff.	P value	Diff.	P value	Diff.	P value	Diff.	P value
Incidence. Months								
Incidence	0.512	0.000	0.195	0.052	0.347	0.000	0.561	0.009
Total months	-0.021	0.053	-0.018	0.175	0.017	0.134	-0.043	0.185
Hostile months	-0.024	0.246	0.005	0.758	-0.026	0.280	0.078	0.206
Episodes								
One	0.448	0.000	0.057	0.620	0.144	0.084	0.288	0.147
Two	0.520	0.000	-0.153	0.530	0.622	0.000	0.378	0.181
Three +	0.388	0.222	0.075	0.869	0.768	0.000	0.569	0.246
Hostile Episodes								
One	-0.239	0.025	0.000	0.998	-0.112	0.174	0.130	0.607
Two	-0.477	0.049	0.432	0.133	-0.107	0.531	0.221	0.686
Three +	0.630	0.412	-0.101	0.842	0.271	0.626	-0.286	0.816

NOTE: Diff. = coefficient for personnel with dependents minus coefficient for personnel without dependents; P value = significance level for rejecting the hypothesis that the difference equals zero.

Asch, Beth J., and John T. Warner, *A Theory of Military Compensation and Personnel Policy*, Santa Monica, Calif.: RAND, MR-439-OSD, 1994.

Buddin, Richard, Daniel S. Levy, Janet M. Hanley, and Donald M. Waldman, *Promotion Tempo and Enlisted Retention*, Santa Monica, Calif.: RAND, R-4135-FMP, 1992.

Compart, Andrew, "Imminent-Danger List Changes Subtract Money for Some," *Army Times*, February 23, 1998.

Cooke, Timothy W., Alan J. Marcus, and Aline O. Quester, *Personnel Tempo of Operations and Navy Enlisted Retention*, CRM-9150, Center for Naval Analysis, February 1992.

Department of Defense, *Military Compensation Background Papers, Fifth Edition*, Office of the Secretary of Defense, U.S. Government Printing Office, Washington, D.C., September 1996.

Department of Defense, Report of the PERSTEMPO Working Group, Washington, D.C.: U.S. Department of Defense, July 12, 1996.

Fossen, Thomas, et al., *What Helps and What Hurts: How Ten Activities Affect Readiness and Quality of Life at Three 8AF Wings*, Santa Monica, Calif: RAND, DB-223-PAF, 1997.

Gotz, Glenn A., and John J. McCall, *A Dynamic Retention Model for Air Force Officers: Theory and Estimates*, Santa Monica, Calif.: RAND, R-3028-AF, 1984.

Greene, William H., *Econometric Analysis, Second Edition*, New York: Macmillan Publishing Company, 1993.

Naylor, Sean D., "Readiness Problems Expected to Continue," *Army Times*, January 5, 1998, p. 18.

Vollrath, LTG Frederick E., Testimony Before Senate Armed Services Subcommittee on Personnel Hearing: FY98 Defense Budget, Washington, D.C., March 5, 1997.

Warner, John T., and Beth J. Asch, "The Economics of Military Manpower," in *Handbook of Defense Economics, Volume 1*, Keith Hartly and Todd Sandler, eds., New York: Elsevier, 1995.

Weible, Jack, "Pentagon to Measure Deployment Tempo," *Army Times*, January 19, 1998, p. 4.